GARDENING WITH WILD PLANTS

JULIAN SLATCHER

THE GUILD OF MASTER CRAFTSMAN
PUBLICATIONS

For Christine Ell – truly the best of friends

First published 2011 by
Guild of Master Craftsman Publications Ltd
Castle Place, 166 High Street, Lewes,
East Sussex BN7 1XU

This title has been created using material
previously published in *Gardening with Wild Plants*
(first published 2000)

ISBN 978-1-86108-803-1

Publisher: Jonathan Bailey
Production Manager: Jim Bulley
Managing Editor: Gerrie Purcell
Senior Project Editor: Virginia Brehaut
Editor: Judith Chamberlain-Webber
Managing Art Editor: Gilda Pacitti
Designer: Chloë Alexander

All photographs by the author, except:
page 11 and 148 Prunella Ashburton-Dunning,
page 19 and 49 (bottom left) Chloë Alexander,
page 73 and 83 (bottom left) thinkstockphotos.com

Set in Nofret and Helvetica Neue
Colour origination by GMC Reprographics
Printed and bound by Hing Yip Printing Co. Ltd

GARDENING
WITH WILD
PLANTS

Contents

Introduction 8

Mixed border plants 13

Rockery, wall and container plants ... 33

Meadow plants 53

Marsh and bog plants 75

Pond plants 95

Hedges and shrubs 115

Shade–loving plants 135

Trees and climbers 155

Further reading/Places to visit 172

Index 173

Introduction

THE WILD plants of Britain are equal in beauty to those of any other land. Who could deny the glory of a bank of snowdrops or daffodils, or the sweet charm of the soft, yellow primrose in spring? What garden isn't richer for containing honeysuckle or bluebells? And what gardener could fail to appreciate the rich green colour and intricate form of a fern, or the hum of bees around a foxglove?

In Britain as in nearly all other nations, the exotic has cast its influence in our gardens. Plants have been brought in from foreign climates to decorate British gardens from the earliest times. The Romans, for example, took plants with them practically wherever they went. Some of the plants brought to Britain were medicinal herbs, some culinary and still others just reminders of a distant homeland. The most noticeable of these imports today is probably that stalwart of English woodlands and parks, the sweet chestnut.

Almost all gardeners use at least some of the innumerable species and varieties that have arrived in our countries in the hands of explorers and plant hunters, or been brought to us by colonizers or conquerers, sometimes even at the expense of our native plants. Despite their great popularity in Britain, for instance, the plants of South Africa were rarely used in the gardens of that country until quite recently: many people there preferred plants that reminded them of Europe, such as roses, delphiniums and foxgloves.

But today we now realize the importance of growing plants in the places where they will be happiest; of using those plants that will thrive in the conditions that we can provide, rather than struggling to keep something alive which does not really belong. Using native plants in the garden is part of adapting to that realization as well as helping us to recall both the wild spaces of our countryside and the origins of the gardening skills for which we, as a nation, have become world renowned.

Introducing wild plants to your garden

GROWING WILD plants in your garden is not hard because luckily there are British native plants that are suitable for almost any position, style or specific requirements you may have from your garden. As more and more nurseries grow and supply them, wild flowers are there to be selected from in the same way as the better-known garden plants, helping to produce the garden that you want, whatever its style.

◀ **Ribbed melilot, ragwort and wild parsley combine to give a splash of cheerful yellow.**

Wild plants for different garden situations

T HERE ARE wild plants that will grow in dry shade, damp shade, full sun, in a mixed or herbaceous border, in a pond or bog garden, on the rockery or in a scree garden, as hedges or specimen shrubs on acid, alkaline, heavy or sandy soil. Before agriculture changed the landscape, it was largely covered in forest, so many plants thrive in shade. Wetland species including ragged robin, purple loosestrife and cotton grass abound in natural marshlands and bogs. Plants suitable for rockeries are found on the barest highlands in Scotland, the Dales, the north Midlands and around the coast. In streams, rivers, ponds and lakes, plants including water lilies, rushes, water soldier and frogbit provide cover and food for wildlife.

Wild plants for different garden styles

W HETHER YOUR garden is formal, informal, cottage, modern or even Mediterranean or Japanese in style, some British wild plants will be suitable. In the Mediterranean garden, strict formality is required, with tightly controlled lines. Box and yew can be clipped readily into whatever shape you require and compact but floriferous plants like the rockrose, thrift, chives, pansies, pinks, knapweed or cornflower can be used in small splashes. A few plants can be added for impact like foxgloves or the martagon lily. In Japanese-style gardens, mosses, ferns, wild cherries, weeping willow and cherry plum are obvious choices, along with box and yew, the saxifrages, water lilies and irises. Even in the most formal garden, wild plants can find a home.

▼ **A front-garden rockery in Pembrokeshire.**

Some of the world's most decorative and useful trees are British natives. In spring there is little to beat the rich orange buds of the black poplar, the pale purity of the whitebeam or the intense green of the lime or field maple. The silver birch is one of the stalwarts of gardens throughout the world and there are numerous varieties of midland hawthorn that have been developed specifically for horticultural use.

If you need ground cover, wild plants can be ideal. Ivy, periwinkles, bugle or sweet violets, the stonecrops and several others will serve readily, blocking out all but the hardiest of weeds. Indeed, some wild flowers are so vigorous that they are best grown in containers in the garden, rather than being allowed to spread at will. The mints and lily of the valley are examples of this.

Using wild plants for all-season interest

IT IS not difficult to achieve an extended season of interest with British wild plants, or even an all-year garden. You can have something in flower from January right through to late autumn, when autumn leaf colour and decorative stems like those of the dogwood, the white-stemmed bramble and yellow-stemmed willows can take over, along with the various berries and variegated evergreen leaves of some varieties of holly, periwinkle, ivy and others, and the rich tones of other evergreens like yew, box or the fascinating, prickly shade-lover – butcher's broom.

In spring, snowdrops and winter aconites are followed by daffodils, lungwort and hellebores along with the new shoots of several trees and shrubs, the flowers of blackthorn and cherry plum and early primroses. Then come the cowslips, bluebells, lily of the valley, red campion and a host of others. These are closely followed by daisies, hawthorn, rowan, alder, cornflowers and saxifrages as well as other meadow and rockery plants. Most plants give of their best through the summer and their season of flowering can be extended by diligent deadheading well into autumn when orpine, ivy, red valerian and cyclamen come into their own.

The pansies and primulas sold by the million every year are descended from the wild field pansy and primrose. They will grow almost wherever you wish to put them, although primulas prefer at least some shade. Primulas can be bought in flower from early winter right through to late spring and pansies will go on flowering for months, if regularly deadheaded. They are often treated as annuals but they are perennial: to give another year of useful life, cut them back hard after flowering.

Using wild plants for a sensory garden

IT IS not just the eye that a garden of British wild flowers can please, but the other senses too. Aspen and silver birch rustle in the slightest breeze, as do taller grasses. Lungwort, hellebores and countless others attract bees and hoverflies through all but the coldest months. Daffodils, lily of the valley, sweet woodruff, scented mayweed, feverfew, sweet violet and meadowsweet are just some of the scented plants we can choose from along with the sweet briar, whose leaves smell of apples on a hot day or when crushed, sweet rocket, mignonette, soapwort and pinks – and who would be without the glorious scent of honeysuckle on a summer evening? Even in the herb garden there are several choices. Thyme, chives, marjoram and mint are all native to the UK, as is the strong-smelling wild garlic, ramsons.

Wild plants for colour

COLOUR CAN be used in a number of ways in the garden. It can affect mood. Green is calming while red is exciting and perhaps a little intimidating in large quantities. Yellow is bright and cheerful, inducing happiness while cooler blues make people feel more reserved and withdrawn. Colour can be used to affect apparent perspective in the garden: red always looks closer while blue looks further away so that grading colours carefully in a border can increase or decrease its apparent length or depth. Colour

▲ **The delicate form of a lady fern.**

can also be used to emphasize the style of a garden. A merry mix will give a cottage–like impression while carefully controlled selections of one, two or three colours can add to the formality and impact of a modern styling.

Conclusion

THE PURPOSE of this book is to re–introduce to the gardening public some of the overlooked gems of the British countryside. These wonderful plants must have been the starting point for Britain's worldwide fame as a nation of gardeners and they still have a valuable place in the garden. Some we already use but do not think of and value as wild plants; others are not commonly seen anymore but add immeasurably to any garden in which they are planted. Space does not allow a comprehensive description here of every British wild plant that has garden potential, but some of those which we cannot describe in detail are mentioned in the chapter introductions and it is not difficult to find fuller details of them in the many books on British wild flowers or on the Internet.

Few British wild plants are exclusive to the UK in their natural distribution. Most also occur across Europe, some even worldwide, so the only restriction on where you can grow them is the conditions that you can provide for them. With use of the Internet, it does not matter where you live – in the UK or abroad – you can still grow a wide range of stunning British wild flowers in your garden.

Julian Slatcher

Mixed borders offer a range of different habitats for growing wild flowers so meadow plants can rub shoulders with shrubs, climbers and shade-lovers. This melting pot needs careful consideration before planting begins, but the mixed border is the one place where normal restrictions do not apply. Almost anything goes here, so you can really be adventurous and creative, and above all have fun while making something uniquely your own.

Mixed border plants

Growing mixed border plants

A MIXED BORDER can be defined as one that includes annuals, perennials and shrubs. The inclusion of shrubs adds structure and form to the planting and maintains at least a modicum of interest through the colder months, when the annuals and most of the perennials have died back. It also means that a variety of different micro–habitats can be formed within the border. There will be little spaces under the edges of shrubs or behind them, as well as between them, which give the plants that are placed there some shelter, if not shade and a drier root-run than they would have had otherwise.

In front of the shrubs, though, is a different habitat. This is more like a meadow situation, where sun–lovers will thrive. Tall plants can be mixed with shorter ones here to give a variation of form and height through the seasons as well as bringing together plants from very different natural environments. This is the place where plants that like damp soil can grow close to those that like dry; plants which like shade can grow with those that like sun and plants which like shelter can grow with those that can tolerate an exposed site. Each protects the others and gives them the conditions that they need.

▼ **Plan for a mixed border in spring.**

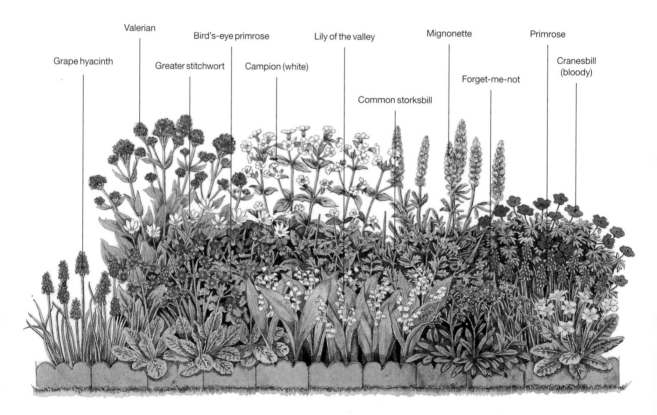

Grape hyacinth · Valerian · Greater stitchwort · Bird's-eye primrose · Campion (white) · Lily of the valley · Common storksbill · Mignonette · Forget-me-not · Primrose · Cranesbill (bloody)

Planning your border

THERE ARE a number of different ways you can choose to arrange the plants in a mixed border. Some opt for the front–to–back slope where tall plants are at the back and short ones at the front so that you can see all at once. Others use an undulating approach with shrubs or other tall plants coming forward towards the front of the border at intervals so that the full length cannot be seen all at once but all is visible from the front. This allows a single border to be segregated into different areas of emphasis in terms of colour theme or planting type. Still others go for the more haphazard look most often associated with a cottage garden.

With the exception of the shrubs and the few plants that are best used as individual statements, the most effective way of arranging plants in a mixed border is in drifts or large, unevenly shaped clumps. This is one case where the adage 'less is more' can be applied, insofar as more impact is obtained by using large quantities of a few species than can be achieved by using small numbers of lots of different plant types. When planted in groups, the full glory of most plants can be appreciated even from a distance. The mixed border is not the place for subtlety in this respect. This can be seen in any of the great gardens. The herbaceous borders of gardens like Wisley in Surrey, Hidcote in Gloucestershire or Newby Hall in Yorkshire among many others all make this point boldly and effectively.

Plant choice

COMBINING PLANTS in a mixed border is part of the fun. Viper's bugloss (p31) can grow in front of columbine (p20), while wild mignonette (p26) or goldenrod (*Solidago virgaurea*) stands tall behind the common mallow (p24) and lady's mantle (p23) can accompany marjoram (p25). Jacob's ladder (p23) can stand behind the field poppy (p68) and toadflax (p31) can shelter

▼ **Plan for a mixed border in early summer.**

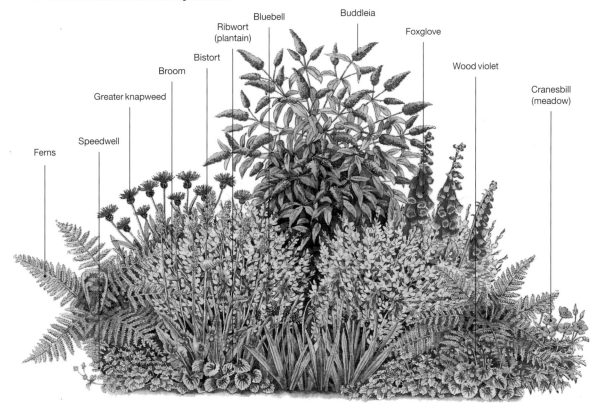

self–heal (p28) while a bold statement can be made through the height of summer with the statuesque yellow–flowered treacle mustard (*Erysimum cheiranthoides*) and culinary as well as decorative use can be made of plants like wild basil (*Clinopodium vulgare*), marjoram and others. Colours can mix and match, with different combinations being separated by shrubs, ferns or grasses, and plants which would not grow anywhere near each other in nature can be combined effectively.

Native climbers including honeysuckle (p164), ivy (p166), the perennial sweet pea (p169), the bryonies and some of the vetches (p72) are as decorative as any imported climber on a wall or trellis but can also be used in the same way as the silvery, red–flowered common fumitory (*Fumaria officinalis*) to weave through the mixed border as scrambling ground–cover. These plants can be combined in the mixed border with early flowering shrubs such as butcher's broom (p121) and mezereon (p128) and bulbs like grape hyacinth (p22), daffodil (p141), martagon lily (*Lilium martagon*) and snake's–head fritillary (*Fritillaria meleagris*), growing over and between them to take up the baton when they have finished flowering.

Growing and propagation

MANY OF the plants mentioned here are available commercially as plugs or potted specimens, though you may have to search for them. And once you have them, the clump formers can be divided every two or three years in spring to make more. Bulbs, once established, can be dug up and thinned every few years; those removed from the clumps being used to make new ones elsewhere. And almost all of the plants you can use in a mixed border are available as seed, which is by far the cheapest and most productive method of introducing new plants to your garden. British native plants have a major advantage in this respect over many of those we more commonly use in the garden: they are, by definition, hardy.

This means that there are three seasons every year when you can sow wildflower seeds for your mixed border: spring, autumn and around the end of the flowering season of the plant

▼ **Plan for a mixed border in mid-summer.**

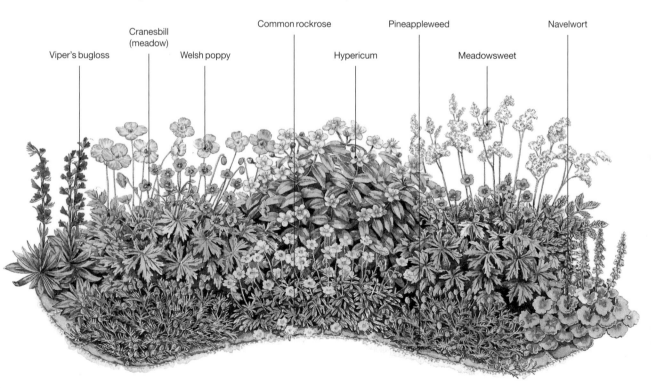

Viper's bugloss Cranesbill (meadow) Welsh poppy Common rockrose Hypericum Pineappleweed Meadowsweet Navelwort

▲ **A mixed border in mid-summer, including foxglove, feverfew, rock rose and ferns.**

Pricking out seedlings

This is best done when their first set of true leaves have just opened out between the seed leaves with which they begin life. You can use a dibber or the end of a pencil to ease them up out of the compost while holding gently by one of the seed leaves. They are then dropped into a pre-formed hole in the compost of their new home and the compost eased in around them. At this stage of their lives, gentle handling is the key. It is only later, when they are fully formed and strong enough to take it that firmer treatment can be employed. Then your new plants can be laid out in the arrangement that you want.

concerned. Another advantage is that no heating is required for germination. In fact many hardy seeds need a period of cold in order to break their dormancy. The best known example of this is probably the primrose, but it is far from unique in this requirement. These seeds are therefore best sown in autumn, but if this is not practical, they can be chilled artificially – given a month or two in the bottom of the fridge, for example. An autumn or late summer sowing will produce sturdy plants that flower a little earlier than spring–sown ones, but sowing in spring allows the ground to be cleared over winter, making it easier to remove weeds. This also helps with plants, such as many of the meadow species, which are best sown where they are to grow rather than in pots or trays for later transplanting. Small seeds can be mixed with dry sand to make it easier to see where you have sown them while larger ones can be placed individually, (although it is often best to place them in pairs so that if one fails, the other can take its place and if both germinate, then a bushier 'plant' results).

If, on the other hand, you are sowing seed in pots or trays, then small seeds just need to sit on the surface of pre–firmed and dampened compost then be covered with polythene or cling film. Larger seeds can be placed individually then pushed down to just below the surface of the compost, which must be kept damp until the plants are pricked out either into their growing positions or into individual pots.

Maintaining a mixed border

It IS a common misconception that if the soil is enriched when growing wild plants, it will promote lots of green growth and cause reduced flowering. But wild plants benefit from feeding and watering as much as any other, so treat them just the same. Pinching out the growing tips cuts out the risk of legginess and increases bushiness and therefore flowering rate. If you do not pinch out the tips of all the plants of a particular species, then you will also extend the flowering season in the same way as deadheading does on most plants.

Polygonum bistorta
Bistort (common)

Description

ALSO KNOWN as knotweed and snakeweed: both of these names, as well as the Latin *bistorta*, refer to its twisted roots. There are several commercially available varieties, many of them bred for the garden from introduced species, mainly from Asia. The young leaves are edible and the long spikes of tiny flowers make a fine display in the garden from May to August. The flowers of the wild species are a soft pink in colour, born in spikes up to 7.5cm (3in) long. They are held high above the leaves on narrow stalks. The leaves are a long oval shape, indented at the base and slightly crinkled in appearance. They look similar to the docks, which they are related to, though smaller, being up to 20cm (8in) long.

How to grow

Height 60cm (24in)
Habitat Likes damp meadows, old scrub and deciduous woods. Can tolerate sun or semi–shade, damp or dry soils.
Garden care Water in well when planting and until established. Cut back to ground level in late autumn, when a mulch of organic matter will be welcomed. Lift and divide clumps every two or three years to keep to required size.
Propagation
Plants and seed are available from nurseries and garden centres. Existing plants can be propagated by division every few years.

▶ **Common bistort (*Polygonum bistorta*)**

Ranunculus ficaria
Celandine (lesser)

Description

THIS MEMBER of the buttercup family grows from small tubers, which put out fibrous roots and smooth stems up to 20cm (8in) long in late winter. The leaves are on long, slender stalks, are roughly heart–shaped, with wavy edges and a shiny dark green colour. Leaves growing from the flower stem are much smaller, with shorter stalks and a more triangular shape. The flowers, borne from February through May, are bright yellow and up to 2.5cm (1in) across, with six to ten narrow petals around a boss of stamens and a green central ovary. The plants can produce long runners that cover a large area, so are best kept confined in containers.

How to grow

Height 15cm (6in)
Habitat Hedge banks, woods and meadows.
Garden care Keep watered through the growing season, which ends soon after flowering is finished in May when the plant dies back. Can be allowed to dry out in summer and brought back again by watering in late winter.
Propagation Plants are available from nurseries and some garden centres. Can be propagated from runners or bulbils formed in the leaf axils.

▼ **Lesser celandine (*Ranunculus ficaria*)**

Allium schoenoprasum
Chives

Description

With its little balls of pink flowers carried on long, slender stalks, this bulbous perennial could be mistaken from a distance for thrift (p49). Closer viewing will reveal the difference, however, for chives do not have the low mat of foliage which is characteristic of thrift. Instead, the tubular, rush–like leaves are almost as long as the flower stalks, which appear over a long period from May through July. Chives form tight tufts of rich green in the mixed border or on the rockery. They are often used as edging in the vegetable garden, where their scent masks that of other plants that are more palatable to garden pests. They look very good edging a path in the ornamental garden, from where the leaves are easy to pick for use in salads, soups or sandwiches or to eat with cheese. Chives are very adaptable, thriving on rich or poor, dry or damp soil. They can happily grow in a pot or trough outside the back door so that their mild onion scent can be enjoyed as you go in and out and they are handy for picking. They are herbaceous, but the leaves come up early in spring and do not die back until early winter, regenerating quickly when cut for use. There are also white–flowered and giant forms available.

How to grow

Height 25cm (10in)
Habitat Found in damp meadows, by riverbanks and along path edges. Can tolerate damp or dry soils; grows best in rich soil, but flowers better in poorer ground. Needs plenty of sun.
Garden care Remove flower stems as the flowers finish. Cut back foliage as it turns yellow with age or in late autumn. Maintenance is minimal; just deadheading and pulling out old, yellowed leaves and dead flower stems as they appear.
Propagation Plants are available from nurseries and garden centres. Clumps can be lifted and divided every two or three years in the spring or autumn.

▼ **Chives (*Allium schoenoprasum*)**

Aquilegia vulgaris
Columbine

Description

ALSO KNOWN as granny's bonnet, the columbine takes its common name from the Latin for dove, describing its bird–like flowers. The native purple form is a plant of open woodland, but has been cultivated for so long that an infinite variety of shades, from white through cream and pale pink to red and purple and almost to black, can be found in gardens all across the British Isles, along with a red–and–white double form, 'Nora Barlow'. The columbines are prolific self–seeders and almost never come true to colour, so any combination of colours may be found in the garden planted with these charming perennials. The leaves are divided into rounded segments, each one usually having three well-defined lobes. They are of a soft greyish–green colour and form a bushy basal rosette in early spring, before the flower stalks rise in May. These have a few leaves, usually less divided and more elliptical in shape, and are branched. There are several to a plant, each branch being topped by one or more flowers from May to July. The seed pods that follow the flowers are narrow, upright and goblet–shaped, opening at the top when ripe and rattling in the wind.

How to grow

Height 50cm (20in)
Habitat Open woodland, grassland, fens and wet woods, usually on lime–rich soil, though this is not essential.
Garden care Water in well when planting, deadhead regularly to prolong flowering and cut down stems in late summer, leaving the basal rosette of leaves into the winter. In mild winters these may remain, otherwise they will die back with the first hard frosts.
Propagation Plants and seeds are available from garden centres and nurseries. The plants rarely come true from seed, with the exception of the double 'Nora Barlow', but the mixtures of colours are very pretty and you will be hard pressed to find one that is not pleasing. Seed can be saved towards the end of the flowering season and sown in pots or trays of compost or where the plants are required in the garden.

◀ Columbine (*Aquilegia vulgaris*)

Geranium sanguineum
Cranesbill (bloody)

Description

ONE OF several pink and red perennial species of hardy geranium, this upright, hairy native has deeply divided leaves and often solitary long–stemmed, cup–shaped flowers of a deep cerise or magenta colour. It begins to flower in May and, with regular deadheading, can be persuaded to continue until well into September. The prominently displayed flowers are about 4cm (1.5in) across, with a long central spire of male and female reproductive parts which turn into the familiar crane's bill fruit. There is a very decorative cultivated form, 'Lancastriense', which has light pink flowers with deep red veining.

How to grow

Height 30cm (12in)
Habitat Grows on dry grassland and scrub, woodland margins, rocky outcrops and dunes but prefers a sunny situation.
Garden care Water in well when planting. Deadhead regularly to prolong flowering. Cut down old stems in late autumn.
Propagation Seed and plants freely available from garden centres and nurseries. Propagate by seed or by division, digging up and splitting the clump in spring or autumn and replanting the new, smaller clumps, watering them in well.

▼ **Bloody cranesbill (*Geranium sanguineum*)**

Chrysanthemum parthenium
Feverfew

Description

AROMATIC FOLIAGE is the main reason for growing this plant. The stems are branched and the leaves light and deeply divided, be they a green–, silver– or yellow–leaved variety. The plant makes a pleasant mound of feathery foliage, which many people keep in the border by clipping off the 2cm (¾in) white-petalled daisy flowers, which appear from July onwards on surprisingly stiff stems. Although it is a perennial, it is often grown as an annual for edging or dot plants in formal bedding displays.

How to grow

Height 10–45cm (4–18in)
Habitat Cornfields, roadsides and waste ground.
Garden care For all its delicate appearance, this is a tough plant. Any normal soil in sun or light shade will suit. Once introduced, feverfew will self-seed freely, so most of the work will be pulling out plants or repositioning them.
Propagation Seed is available from garden centres and nurseries and is best sown in early spring. Plants can be bought later in the season, although the green-leaved variety is usually only available from more specialist wild-flower nurseries. Semi-ripe cuttings can be taken in late summer and rooted in pots in a cool, shady place. Seed can be collected from plants, if allowed to flower.

◀ **Feverfew (*Chrysanthemum parthenium*)**

Muscari neglectum
Grape hyacinth

Description

THIS IS a bulbous plant with slightly succulent grass-like leaves, which are almost evergreen. A dense spike of blue flowers is produced on stems up to about 20cm (8in) long in April or May. Each flower is small and cup-like, hanging downward. Modern garden varieties often have larger flowers than the wild plant, and are sometimes a deeper blue. A white-flowered variety is also available commercially.

How to grow

Height 22cm (9in)
Habitat Meadows or open woodland, often on chalk soils.
Garden care It is best planted in autumn. Prefers well-drained soil and sun.
Propagation Bulbs can be bought from a garden centre or nursery, though these are often of related species rather than this native one. A similar native species, which is available commercially, is the small grape hyacinth (*M. botryoides*). This is slightly smaller than the grape hyacinth and has sky-blue flowers. Clumps should be divided every few years.

▼ Grape hyacinth (*Muscari neglectum*)

Campanula rotundifolia
Harebell

Description

CLOSELY RELATED to the other bellflowers, mentioned elsewhere in this chapter, the harebell is a truly lovely plant which should be included in any sunny garden. Confusingly known as the bluebell in Scotland, its 2.5cm (1in), pale blue bell flowers are displayed from June through to September. Although the flowers are nodding, the tight buds are upright on the fine stems. The stem leaves, mainly towards the bottoms of the many stems, are long and narrow, and pale green like the stems. The basal leaves that are present in early spring before the flowering stems rise, are long-stalked, little tooth-edged circles. Overall, this is a delicate, dainty-looking gem of a perennial.

How to grow

Height 50cm (20in)
Habitat Meadows, dry grassland and scree slopes.
Garden care Water it in well, but it should not need watering again once established. Keep slugs at bay and deadhead to improve flowering.
Propagation Plants and seed are available from specialist nurseries. Seed can be saved from existing plants and sown in pots or where it is to flower in autumn so that it germinates in spring, after the cold of winter.

◀ Harebell (*Campanula rotundifolia*)

Polemonium caeruleum
Jacob's ladder

Description

THIS USEFUL border perennial is a native of most of Europe, including the British Isles, and has been cultivated in gardens since at least Roman times. There are several forms, but generally it is an upright plant with finely divided pinnate leaves in a rich, dark green colour and rich blue, five-petalled flowers with golden stamens displayed prominently from their centres. It is the leaves that give the plant its name, the leaflets being narrow and rung-like, but it is the flowers for which it is grown in the garden. They begin to open in May and will continue throughout the summer. Cultivated forms include a white variant, large-leaved scrambling ones, some with blue flowers, others with pale pink, and several larger-flowered ones.

How to grow

Height 60cm (24in)
Habitat Likes dry grassland and hillsides. Will grow in any soil type, in sun or partial shade.
Garden care Add compost to the soil when planting and deadhead regularly to prolong flowering. Provide support and cut down the stems in autumn.
Propagation Seed and plants are freely available in garden centres and nurseries. Once established, the plants should self-seed freely. Best propagated from seed.

▶ Jacob's ladder (*Polemonium caeruleum*)

Alchemilla vulgaris
Lady's mantle

Description

THERE ARE several closely related species of lady's mantle, many of them introduced down the centuries for garden use. All look very similar, though some are smaller or more upright than others. They have light green palmate leaves with toothed edges which are softly hairy so that they retain drops of water on their upper surface after rain. The flowers are born in soft, branching panicles which look like yellow froth above the round, lobed leaves from May to September. This hardy perennial is almost evergreen, retaining at least a few leaves through the winter.

How to grow

Height 45cm (18in)
Habitat Grows best in damp shade but will tolerate drier and sunnier conditions.
Garden care Water in well, as you would any other plant, but very little looking after will be needed from then on. Just cut away dead leaves and deadhead, more to prevent excess self-seeding than to extend the flowering season.
Propagation Most plants sold (unless you go to more specialist nurseries) are of *Alchemilla mollis* – an introduced species which makes an equally good garden subject. The plant should self-seed around the garden. You can also lift and divide the plants every two or three years.

▼ Lady's mantle (*Alchemilla vulgaris*)

Malva
Mallow

Description

A BRIGHT, CHEERY green plant, standing up to 1.2m (4ft) tall, though it is herbaceous, unlike the garden varieties that are so commonly available. (These, however, are best cut down almost to ground level in early spring, as you would roses.) The mallow is covered in pink flowers, 5–7cm (2–2¾in) across, throughout the summer. It can make a bold statement if allowed room in the garden, but can take a little crowding. In these conditions some of the stems fall flat to the ground and spread out to smother the competition, while others stay upright.

There are several mallows native to Britain, all usually found in the southern counties. Common mallow (*M. sylvestris*) is a tall plant, reaching 1m (3ft) or so. Its leaves are much less divided, almost palmate in appearance, the flowers darker, petals narrower and separated, the tips divided. Often there is a purple marking near the base of the petals, sometimes forming a stripe down their length. The leaves are edible and can be used in salads. The musk mallow (*M. moschata*) gets its name from the smell the plant gives off when in a warm place, especially noticeable if it is used as a cut flower. Large-flowered mallow (*M. alcea*) has leaves similar to those of the musk mallow, but flowers more like those of the common mallow. Dwarf mallow (*M. neglecta*) has five-lobed, undivided leaves and pale-pink, purple-striped flowers about 2cm (¾in) across. Its stems grow to 60cm (24in) and trail along the ground. Marsh mallow (*Althea officinalis*) is a velvety-grey plant with pink flowers up to 2.5cm (1in) across.

How to grow

Height 1m (3ft)
Habitat With the exception of the now quite rare marsh mallow, all the mallows like dry, sunny locations such as field edges, roadsides and meadowland.
Garden care Given plenty of sun, mallows can tolerate most soil conditions and some crowding.
Propagation Seed is available from some nurseries and garden centres, and plants are becoming more widely available. Once you have a plant, the seeds are easy to collect, the fruit being in the form of curled 'nutlets'. The nuts can be split and the seed inside them sown in gritty compost in late summer or spring.

▼ **Musk mallow (*Malva moschata*)**

▼ **Common mallow (*Malva sylvestris*)**

Origanum vulgare
Marjoram

Description

THE AROMATIC leaves of this hairy plant are used to make a herb tea, while an oil extracted from it was once used as a painkiller. This is not, however, the marjoram used in the kitchen: that is a Mediterranean species, *O. onites*. Marjoram is usually found growing wild in dry grassland, open woodland and sunny hedgerows, often on lime–rich soil. It blooms from June to September. There is a golden–leaved variety, golden marjoram (*O. vulgare* 'Aureum') which flowers less prolifically and over a shorter period, from August to September, but is highly decorative simply for its leaves.

How to grow

Height 60cm (24in)
Habitat Dry, sunny grassland and woodland edges.
Garden care Marjoram is related to the mints, though it is less invasive, and needs similar treatment. Grows well in pots or window boxes or as a front–of–border plant. Benefits from cutting back quite hard after flowering to keep the plant fresh.
Propagation Plants can be found in many garden centres and nurseries. Pot–grown plants can be planted out from spring through to autumn. Established plants in the garden can be lifted and divided in spring.

► **Marjoram (*Origanum vulgare*)**

Astrantia major
Masterwort

Description

A MEMBER OF the carrot family, though you would not think so from the exotic-looking flower heads, this stately plant has long been popular in gardens. There is a large range of cultivars available, some with variegated leaves, others with flowers anything from white through green to deepest burgundy red. The flowers are about 2.5cm (1in) across, at the tops of branching narrow stems with deeply cut leaves. They are surrounded by a sunray of papery, pointed bracts, the natural form being a pinkish green colour with pale pink centres. It's one of our oldest cottage garden plants.

How to grow

Height 1m (3ft)
Habitat Found on meadows and scrubland, mainly on chalky soil. Does well in partial shade.
Garden care Water in well when planting and again if the weather turns hot and dry. Keep watch for slugs, especially in spring, when the new shoots are emerging from the ground, and stake in exposed situations.
Propagation Plants and seed are available from garden centres and nurseries. Seed can be saved from existing plants in the garden and sown in pots or trays in the spring. Plants can be lifted and divided every three years or so in spring or autumn.

▼ **Masterwort (*Astrantia major*)**

Reseda lutea
Mignonette (wild)

Description

SIMILAR IN appearance to garden mignonette (*R. odorata*), which comes originally from North Africa, wild mignonette lacks the rich scent of its garden relative, but is still useful as a subtle backing to plants such as thymes or speedwells in the mixed border or rockery. It is an upright plant with greyish–green leaves finely cut into linear segments, and greenish–yellow flowers in long racemes from May to October. Weld (*R. luteola*) is a closely related plant, similar in appearance and habitat, but larger and with undivided lanceolate leaves and a longer inflorescence. Weld grows as a biennial, whereas mignonette is a short–lived perennial.

How to grow

Height 60cm (24in)
Habitat Occurs naturally by roadsides, waste ground and on grassy slopes. Often found on disturbed ground, especially on chalk or limestone in the south and east of England.
Garden care Choose a sunny spot, add lime if the soil is acid and deadhead regularly as the flower spikes finish.
Propagation Available from some specialist nurseries as seed. Sow where it is to flower in mid to late summer, rake in lightly and water well, then leave it to its own devices. Seed can be saved from existing plants and sown in the same way.

▶ **Wild mignonette (*Reseda lutea*)**

Aconitum napellus
Monkshood

Description

BY FAR the most common of our two native monkshoods, the other being *A. anglicum*, a rare plant of south–west England with lilac–blue flowers in May and June. Monkshood is also called wolfsbane for the poison that was extracted from its roots and used to tip the arrows of hunters in the Middle Ages. The glossy leaves are dark green, fan–shaped and deeply divided. The flowers, displayed from June into August on branching spikes, are deep blue and hooded. White– and pink–flowered varieties are also available. All parts of the plant are poisonous, so wear gloves when handling it.

How to grow

Height 1m (3ft)
Habitat Favours damp woods and streams, up to quite high altitudes. Can tolerate sun or shade, but needs some moisture in the soil.
Garden care Water in well when planting and ensure that it does not dry out in summer. Deadhead as flower spikes become spent, then cut down to ground level in late autumn. A mulch of well–rotted garden compost or farmyard manure at this time of year is a good idea.
Propagation Plants and seed are available from nurseries and garden centres. Seed can be saved and sown in pots outside in late summer. Plants can be lifted and divided in spring or autumn, every few years.

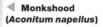
◀ **Monkshood (*Aconitum napellus*)**

Campanula trachelium
Nettle-leaved bellflower

Description

WHEN NOT in flower this upright, hairy plant looks very like a nettle. It can grow to 1m (3ft) tall, but often settles for half that or less, especially in a good, sunny situation. The lower leaves have longer stalks than the upper ones, all are triangular in shape and double–toothed like a nettle, and the stiff stems are angular in section. But with the arrival of midsummer, identification suddenly becomes easy, for the flower buds, held in loose, terminal and near–terminal panicles, begin to open. The flowers are a rich blue, with the classic bell shape of the campanulas and up to 4cm (1.5in) long, opening from late June to September. At this time they furnish a handsome contrast to some of the hotter colours that are prominent in the summer garden. The plant grows well, for instance, with yellow loosestrife (*Lysimachia vulgaris*) and bloody cranesbill (*Geranium sanguineum*).

How to grow

Height 1m (3ft)
Habitat Naturally found in deciduous woodland, hedges and scrub. It is tolerant of sun or shade, though it prefers drier soils.
Garden care Cut back flower spikes when they have finished to encourage further flowering. Cut back to ground level in late autumn. A mulch with bark chippings, leaf mould or well–rotted manure after cutting back at the end of the season is welcome.
Propagation Plants are available from garden centres. Existing plants can be lifted and divided every three years in spring or autumn. Seed can be saved and sown in pots or trays outside in summer, though they will not germinate until after a significant cold spell, such as they would naturally experience through the winter.

▲ ▶ **Nettle-leaved bellflower (Campanula trachelium)**

Eryngium maritimum
Sea holly

Description

THIS BRANCHED perennial, along with its more slender and branched cousin field holly (*Eryngo E. campestre*), grows from a basal rosette of smooth–edged, long, slim, ovoid leaves. The stem leaves, however, are vastly different. Stiff, curled and with many large spines around the edge, these are what give the sea holly its name. The stems begin to rise in spring, growing and branching and eventually forming rosettes of spines at their tips, in the centres of which are formed the flower heads. These are rounded or oval, up to 5cm (2in) long and usually bluish in colour when they open from July to September. Makes a spectacular statement in the border.

How to grow

Height 30–60cm (12–24in)
Habitat Sandy soils, dunes and shingle beaches, usually on the coast, though it will thrive in any well–drained neutral or alkaline soil. Likes full sun.
Garden care Water in when planting but should not need further watering. Cut back stems to ground level in late autumn.
Propagation Plants and seed are available from garden centres and nurseries, along with several introduced species. Plants can be carefully divided every few years, but do not like root disturbance.

▼ **Sea holly (*Eryngium maritimum*)**

Prunella vulgaris
Self-heal

Description

THE SQUARISH stems of this perennial herb, often a pinkish–green colour, rise from short rhizomes. They bear light green, elliptical leaves in widely spaced pairs, one pair of which is found tight to the base of the short flower spike. All of the flowers in any spike will never be found to be out at once. Self–heal forms a thick clump of buds, seed heads and open, hooded flowers, very similar to those of the mints and sages, to which it is related. Very variable in size, according to where it is grown, the self–heal has long been cultivated in gardens. There are white–flowered and variegated–leaved varieties available as well as the natural violet–flowered type.

How to grow

Height 5–35cm (2–14in), depending on competition for light and moisture as well as grazing or clipping.
Habitat Meadows, scrubland and woods but will grow in sun or shade, on damp or dry ground.
Garden care Water in well when planting, but this should not be needed after the plant has settled. Deadhead when a spike is fully over. Look out for blackspot on the leaves and pick off affected ones, burning them or throwing them in the dustbin.
Propagation Plants and seed are available from nurseries and garden centres. Seed can be saved from existing plants and sown in pots in late summer. Plants can be lifted and divided every few years.

◀ **Self-heal (*Prunella vulgaris*)**

Jasione montana
Sheep's-bit

Description

D ESPITE THE fact that it looks like a scabious
and is sometimes called sheep's scabious, it
is not. Instead it is classified as a member of the
bellflower family. It has a rosette of toothed,
narrow leaves from which several almost leafless
flowering stems rise in late spring. The tiny deep–
blue flowers, clustered into scabious–like button
heads about 4cm (1½in) across, open from June to
August. A perennial plant, it looks very pretty in
the sun at the front of a border, combined with
one of the knapweeds or poppies.

How to grow

Height Up to 60cm (24in), but often much
smaller, depending on competition for light
Habitat Favours dry grassland, cliff tops and
the edges of pine woods. Can tolerate neutral
to alkaline soils. Prefers some moisture, but
not too much.
Garden care Water in well when planting and
again if the weather turns hot and dry for
an extended period. Deadhead to extend the
flowering period. Mulch in autumn with well–
rotted garden compost or manure. Stake if grown
tightly among other plants, so that it grows tall.
Propagation Plants and seed are available from
specialist nurseries and occasionally some
garden centres. Seed can be saved from existing
plants and sown in pots outside in autumn to
germinate in the
following spring.

Veronica spicata
Speedwell (spiked)

Description

A LTHOUGH THIS is the most commonly grown
species of native speedwell in our gardens
by far, it is the rarest in the wild and, as such,
is a protected species. There are many varieties
which have been bred for the garden, varying
from white through pale and dark blues to pink
and even dark red flowers, though the natural
form has sky–blue blooms from June to August.
It has long, rounded leaves, opposite on the stem
and downy with toothed edges. These get smaller
as they get higher up the stem towards the base
of the long, slender flower spike, of which there
can be several to a plant. The flowers are tiny but
too numerous to count, the spike thick and up to
30cm (12in) long.

How to grow

Height 60cm (24in)
Habitat Pastures, sunny slopes and rocky places,
usually in milder regions.
Garden care Once established in a warm, sunny
site, little care is needed. Deadhead when flower
spikes are spent and mulch in spring or autumn.
Propagation Plants and seed are available from
nurseries and some garden centres. Existing plants
can be lifted and divided in spring or autumn.

▼ **Spiked speedwell (*Veronica spicata*)**

▶ **Sheep's-bit
(*Jasione montana*)**

Hypericum sp.
St John's wort

Description

THERE ARE around 400 species of St John's wort, distributed from Ireland to Japan. Some are shrubby, like the European and Chinese introductions commonly used in our gardens; others are evergreen herbs; still others are herbaceous perennials, as Britain's 14 native species tend to be. Of these, common or perforate St John's wort (*H. perforatum*) is probably the most widespread, growing from England's south coast to the Scottish Highlands. It is distinguished by having clear, translucent spots, filled with oil, on the long, oval leaves, and black spots on the petals and flower stalks. It grows up to 1m (3ft) tall, with many leafy branches and the flowers, up to 2.5cm (1in) across, are borne in terminal branched clumps from June to September.

Square-stalked St John's wort (*H. tetrapterum*), pictured, is up to 60cm (24in) high, with more oblong leaves, no spotting and larger, fewer flowers. It tends to grow in damp places. Trailing St John's wort (*H. humifusum*) is a small, trailing plant, the stems rarely more than 15cm (6in) long, whose flowers do not open in bad weather. It is often found on acid heaths, along with slender St John's wort (*H. pulchrum*), which is a larger plant, up to 60cm (24in) tall. Taller again, at around 1m (3ft), and an acid hater like the common species, is hairy St John's wort (*H. hirsutum*), which has hairs on both sides of the small, narrow leaves and pale yellow flowers through July and August. This species tends to be found in damp woodland and scrub.

There is a St John's wort for most situations in the garden, bearing bright yellow flowers with prominent bunches of pretty stamens throughout the summer months.

How to grow

Height Most species grow to 30–100cm (12–36in), with the exception of the trailing one, which rarely exceeds 15cm (6in) and is ideal for a rockery or container.

Habitat Each has its own niche: some like wet ground, some dry, some acid, some limy. Check specific details when making your selection.

Garden care Water in well when planting, deadhead thoroughly to prolong flowering and cut down stems of herbaceous species in late autumn. An organic mulch in winter will help give vigour to the plants in the following year. Plants can contract fungal diseases, such as black spot or rust, and affected leaves should be removed and destroyed as soon as this is noticed.

Propagation Native species are available from nurseries as plants or seed. Seed should be sown in pots or trays outside, the plants placed into their flowering positions in late spring. Cuttings can be taken in summer and rooted in pots of compost, sealed into a plastic bag.

◀ **St John's wort (*Hypericum sp.*)**

Linaria vulgaris
Toadflax (common)

Description

THIS USUALLY 30cm (12in) perennial has bright yellow, snapdragon–like flowers with a long, nectar–filled spur on the back of the lower lip. These are carried in a short spike at the top of the slim stem. Narrow grey–green leaves grow up the stem to the base of the flower spike. The flowering season extends from June to October and, like many plants, can be extended by deadheading. Toadflax enjoys sun, but is strong enough to withstand close competition in a short–cropped meadow environment. A tight bunch of it would also look excellent on a rockery, perhaps with heartsease (*Viola tricolor*) and a gentian.

How to grow

Height 60cm (24in)
Habitat Short grassland, roadside verges and field edges.
Garden care Grow in full sun for best results. Partial shade can be tolerated, but the plants tend to be taller and weaker.
Propagation Best sown where it is to flower, either in autumn or early spring. Each plant will spread a little by underground rhizomes, but seed is easy to collect once you have the plants. Plants and seed are available from specialist nurseries. Garden centres tend to stock the very similar but multi–coloured foreign varieties, which are annuals.

▶ **Common toadflax (*Linaria vulgaris*)**

Echium vulgare
Viper's bugloss

Description

NAMED FOR the shape of its seeds, this hairy member of the borage family grows up to 1m (3ft), over half of which is taken up by the long flower spike from early June to late September. The plant grows as a biennial, in the first year producing a rosette of dark-green, 20cm (8in) leaves covered with stiff hairs. In the second year a bristly stem rises, with smaller leaves growing ladder–wise from it, getting smaller as they near the top. It is from the axils of these that the flowers come. These are red in bud opening to a rich blue with prominent reddish stamens, each flower a 2cm (¾in) bell with an irregular lip.

How to grow

Height 1m (3ft)
Habitat Likes open dry grassland and downs, waste ground, quarries and headlands. Prefers chalky or limestone soils.
Garden care Water in well when planting, give the plant space and light and cut down the flowering stems when they have finished. When handling the plant wear gloves, as it has many tiny, hair–like spines.
Propagation Seed and plants are available from nurseries. Seed can be saved from existing plants, but if the plant is allowed to seed it will die.

◀ **Viper's bugloss (*Echium vulgare*)**

Whether you are building a new rockery, creating
a raised bed, adding interest to a wall or patio or
filling a few tubs or troughs, all these situations
are ideally suited to native rockery plants. As long
happy, you will be
play in the colour
And with the right
y can go on from
ough to October.

ery,
wall and
container
plants

Growing in small spaces

Y OU DO not need to build a rockery in order to enjoy rockery plants. Indeed, you do not even need a sunny site, as several are very tolerant of shade. Any free–draining position will do, however restricted the root-run. The cracks between the slabs of a patio are ideal, especially for plants that give off scent when

trodden on or brushed past, like feverfew (p21), lawn chamomile (p60) or thyme (p50). Mosses, stonecrops, navelwort (p42) or Welsh poppies (p147) can gain the tiniest of footholds in the crevices of an old wall. A drive through the lanes of Cornwall or west Wales will reveal some of the more incongruous–seeming possibilities for plants that will tolerate and even thrive in the free–draining, sunny conditions of the classic rockery situation.

▼ **Plan for a rockery in early summer.**

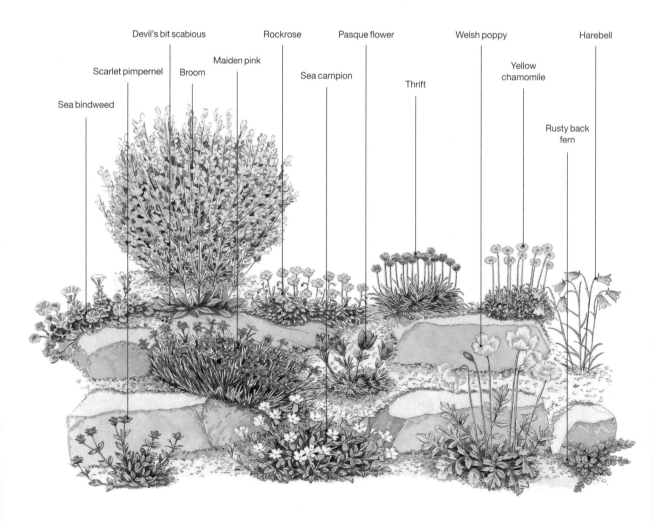

Rockeries

T HE MORE usual approach, however, is to employ the spoil from the digging of a pond, bog–garden or even patio as the basis of a rockery. The rockery is something that was overdone and often badly done in the 1960s and 1970s, so that now it is distinctly out of fashion.

The trick with a rockery is to make it look as if it belongs, so you need to use careful shaping to blend it in with its surroundings. It may be that some form of support is required at the back in the form of upright stakes driven into the ground close to a fence or wall or it may be that a gentle slope can lead back from a steeper front face. Parts of it can be hidden with shrubs or blended in with grass and, if placed next to a pond, it may be that the front can be employed as the support

Choosing plants

When it comes to choosing plants, do not buy anything 'just to fill a gap', as you can be sure that something will fill it for you by next year. Think about shapes, textures, leaf types and flowering times as well as the size of the mature plants. It is not something that design students are willing to admit, but it is very difficult to achieve a plant combination that clashes, so do not worry about that.

▼ **Plan for a late-season rockery.**

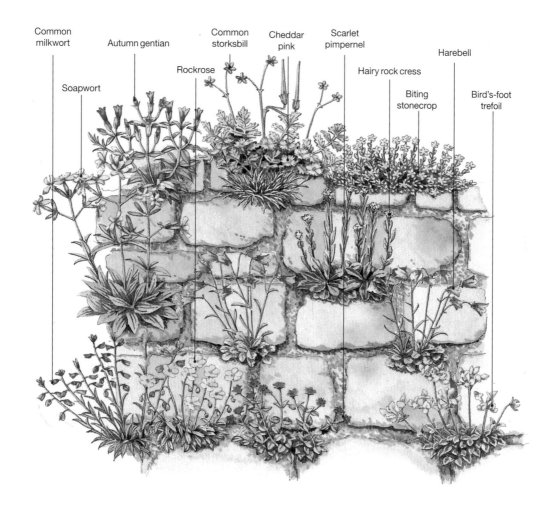

Common milkwort

Autumn gentian

Common storksbill

Cheddar pink

Scarlet pimpernel

Harebell

Rockrose

Hairy rock cress

Soapwort

Biting stonecrop

Bird's-foot trefoil

Walls

AN INCREASINGLY popular way of enlarging potential plant space is to leave a planting channel in the top of a garden wall. Many of the plants mentioned in this chapter and some others would be perfectly happy in such a position and it is not difficult to create. Any wall that is wide enough can have two lines of stone or brick cemented along the top with a channel left between them. This channel is then lined with polythene that has had plenty of drainage holes punched through it with a hand-fork. The resulting trough is filled with a gritty mix of compost, preferably a John Innes type with some body to it rather than the lighter multi-purpose types, then planted up with a mix of rockery plants, grasses (p62), dwarf shrubs like heather (p126), bearberry (*Arctostaphylos Uva-Ursi*) and rockrose (p44), or scented herbs like marjoram (p25) and thyme (p50).

The arrangement of the plants is a matter of personal taste. Using two or three varieties in repetition such as creeping bellflower (p38) with just a few clumps of wood meadow grass can be highly effective or you can go for the multi-colour effect with one each of several different species, either of all the same height or mixing taller ones like the bright pink sticky catchfly (*Lychnis viscaria*) which grows up to 60cm (24in) tall with the low-growing bright yellow of biting stonecrop (p48), the contrasting darkness of perhaps a purple-leaved variety of the blue-flowered bugle (*Ajuga reptans*) and even the delicately veined white variety of the common storksbill (*Erodium cicutarium*). This is also the perfect spot for the dry-ground species of gentian, such as the spring gentian (*Gentiana verna*), the fringed gentian (*G. cilliata*) and the purplish flowered autumn gentian (*G. amarella*).

▼ **Plan for patio slabs in mid-summer.**

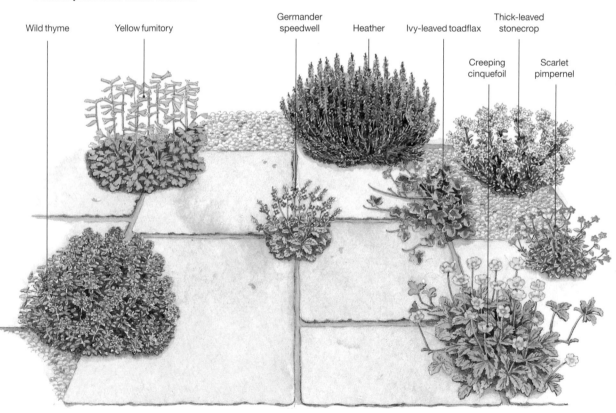

Wild thyme   Yellow fumitory   Germander speedwell   Heather   Ivy-leaved toadflax   Thick-leaved stonecrop

Creeping cinquefoil   Scarlet pimpernel

for a waterfall. In this case, the top of the mound behind the waterfall can provide the ideal place to conceal the pond filter box, which can be sunk into the earth and covered with a stone, a planting trough or even a piece of turf. It should be borne in mind though that you will need access to the filter box at least once a year in order to clean it out.

Visit local successful examples or places where the conditions you are trying to replicate occur naturally such as local rocky outcrops, cliffs, long–abandoned quarries, ruins or sand-banks and see what plants are growing and how the rock sits in the land. How much or how little is exposed, how the grain lies, how worn or jagged it is and how each stone relates to its neighbours can all be replicated in the garden and the plants you see can give the basis for a wider-ranging planting scheme, as you know that they will thrive in your conditions. Take pictures so that you have an immediate reminder when you get back to your own site. These things are not easy to get right even when you have a sloping garden to start with, but it can be done with a little care and thought and a great deal of muscle power.

Using hyper-tufa
Though the use of wild plants in the garden enhances the natural beauty of the plot, it is essentially artificial. It is also possible to manufacture extremely realistic artificial 'rocks' rather than use real ones from a quarry. This innovative method was developed by the late British gardener Geoff Hamilton. First, dig a hole in a spare patch of ground, in the size and rough shape of the 'rock' required. Line it with polythene, the thicker the better, as the creases and folds are used to good effect. Smother it with a stiff mix of cement to which has been added soil or compost. The mix, which Geoff Hamilton called hyper–tufa, should consist of one part of cement to four parts sharp sand and one part of compost or fine soil. If the mix is sufficiently stiff, the hole need not be filled completely, the mix being able to be pushed up against the sides so that the resulting 'rock' will be hollow – an advantage as it will not be too heavy to move into position. Let the 'rock' set completely, then lift it

Stone sinks

Hyper-tufa can also be used to create a 'stone' sink. You can cover an old ceramic sink with PVA glue, allow it to go tacky, then cover it with hyper-tufa, or you can form a suitable mould from wood and polythene and fill it using the same method as for making a rock.

out of the hole. Remove the polythene, which can be re-used to make further 'rocks' of the same or completely different shapes. Old compost bags are good for this, but do not split them into single layers: the more creased they are the better and the double layer enhances this effect.

Containers

EVEN THE most artificial of planting environments has its uses when growing wildflowers. It is well known that the mints will spread quickly and, if they are allowed to do so, will take over a large area of ground. A good way to confine them is by planting them in a container, which can then be sunk into the ground. If you are gardening in a confined space, the same rule applies to lily of the valley. If this plant likes the soil, it will spread vigorously by underground rhizomes, and can be difficult to confine.

We all enjoy expanding the capacity of our gardens with pots, tubs, hanging baskets and other containers. Many native plants, including primroses, pansies – especially the smaller varieties – and many bulbs, are suitable for this style of growing, and can provide a welcome splash of colour. Equally useful are speedwell (p47), common storksbill, common fumitory (*Fumaria officinalis*) and yellow fumitory, sea campion (p39), common toadflax (p31), bird's-foot trefoil (p38), creeping bellflower (p38) and wood sorrel (p150). In fact, most rockery plants will do well in containers.

Campanula patula

Bellflower (creeping)

Description

CLOSELY RELATED to the harebell and the other bellflowers, the creeping bellflower is not common in the wild, but has found a niche in our gardens. Its open, pale–blue, five–petalled flowers are about 2.5cm (1in) across and fairly cover the plant for about three months at the height of summer. Of all the bellflowers, it is most similar in appearance to the harebell (p22), with its pale flowers, slender stems and tight, long buds. Also the leaves are similar, the basal leaves stalked and spoon shaped while those further up the lax stems are narrow and lanceolate. The plant will spread to form quite substantial mats of foliage if allowed and will self–seed freely.

How to grow

Height 60cm (24in)
Habitat Meadows, waste ground and scrub.
Garden care Once planted and watered in, it should not need further watering unless grown in containers. Excessive growth can simply be pulled or clipped away to keep the plant within the bounds you have allowed in the garden.
Propagation Plants and seed are available from garden centres and nurseries. Seed can be saved or allowed to self sow. Clumps can be lifted and divided every two or three years.

Lotus corniculatus

Bird's-foot trefoil

Description

A PRETTY LITTLE plant which has bright yellow, pea–like flowers about 1cm (½in) long, reddish when in bud. It can happily hug the ground on footpaths, growing no more than 2.5cm (1in) high, or it can attain 35cm (14in) in longer grass, where it tends to grow in the company of plants such as sainfoin (p70) and ox–eye daisy (p66). It looks trifoliate, but in fact there are five lobes to each leaf, three of them at the end of a short stalk, the other two at its base. The name comes from the fruit, which is 2cm (¾in) long, chestnut brown when ripe and spread out like a bird's foot. The flowers appear from May until the autumn frosts, but mainly in June and July.

How to grow

Height Varies from 2.5–35cm (1–14in), depending on situation.
Habitat Dry grassland, meadows and footpaths.
Garden care Provide a well–drained, sunny aspect and this plant will look after itself either as a specimen on the rockery or in a meadow.
Propagation Scarification, or scratching of the seed helps germination, as with all the pea family. Seed can then be broadcast or sown in pots for later transplantation.

▼ Bird's-foot trefoil (*Lotus corniculatus*)

▶ Creeping bellflower (*Campanula patula*)

Silene uniflora
Campion (sea)

Description

OFTEN REGARDED as a sub–species of the erect, 60cm (24in) bladder campion (*S. vulgaris*) of roadsides and downland, the sea campion is very similar with white flowers backed by broad, ovoid bladders, but it's much shorter with fleshier leaves and a low, cushion-shaped habit. The branching stems of both types are greyish in colour, the narrow ovoid leaves greyish green, as are the bladder–like calices behind the flowers, though these are sometimes pinkish white. The flowers of the sea campion, about 2cm (¾in) across, are often borne singly on their slender stems, unlike those of the bladder campion, which are in loose bunches on stems that divide repeatedly into threes. These plants will flower from May to September and will grow in the poorest of conditions.

How to grow

Height 15cm (6in)
Habitat Cliff tops, ledges, shingle and grassland.
Garden care Water in when planting, choosing a sunny site. Deadhead regularly to keep the plant looking tidy.
Propagation Seed and plants are available from nurseries and garden centres. Seed can be saved towards the end of the flowering season and sown in gritty compost in pots or trays outside or where the plants are required.

▶ **Sea campion
(*Silene uniflora*)**

Centaurium erythraea
Centaury (common)

Description

ALTHOUGH IT has a similar name to the knapweeds, this pink–flowered biennial is more closely related to the gentians. Its smooth, light–green stems rise from a basal rosette of oval leaves and bear shiny, pointed elliptical leaves in pairs, up to the point where they branch into a loose umbel–like arrangement to be topped by the starry, yellow–centred pink flowers. The flowering season is from July to September. Like many plants, the common centaury is very variable in size, according to its growing conditions. Competition for light and moisture can create a plant anything from 5–45cm (2–18in) high, with one or many stems, but however large it gets, the flowers are a pretty sight in the sun and it makes a good companion to more substantial plants, such as the knapweeds, campions or geraniums.

How to grow

Height Up to 45cm (18in)
Habitat Sunny dry meadows and grassy slopes.
Garden care In common with some other biennials, plants can be saved for another year of flowering if they are not allowed to set seed.
Propagation Sow seeds in summer and overwinter plants in pots for planting out in spring or in their flowering position. Plants and seed are available from specialist nurseries.

◀ **Common centaury (*Centaurium erythraea*)**

Potentilla reptans
Cinquefoil (creeping)

Description

BRIGHT YELLOW, five-petalled flowers up to 2.5cm (1in) across stand up above the strawberry-like, ground-hugging leaves of this trailing sun-lover. The stems stretch up to 22cm (9in) across the ground, rooting occasionally at the leaf axils, with leaves and flowers being borne in groups along the stem. The compound leaves, made of five centrally attached, toothed leaflets, give the plant its common name from the Norman French. A good plant for trailing over rocks or as a filler between other low-growing plants. A similar plant is the four-petalled tormentil (*P. erecta*). More inclined to be erect and tufted, it also makes a good rockery plant, but it will not thrive on calcareous soils.

How to grow

Height 5–10cm (2–4in)
Habitat Banks and roadsides in short grassland.
Garden care Stems can be cut back in autumn after flowering. The leaves can contract a brown rust disease, especially if growing in shady or damp areas. This can be treated by removal of the affected leaves if caught early, otherwise a fungicide spray will be necessary.
Propagation Seed and plants are available from specialist nurseries. Once established, pegging down the stems at intervals will encourage stem rooting, after which new plants can be cut away.

▶ **Creeping cinquefoil (*Potentilla reptans*)**

Geranium molle
Cranesbill (dove's-foot)

Description

SMALL, PINK flowers roughly 2cm (¾in) across adorn this annual through June and July, sitting in pairs or singly above shallowly cut, almost-round leaves. It is one of three annual cranesbills native to these shores, probably the most common of which is the cut-leaved cranesbill (*G. dissectum*). This has deeply divided leaves and darker, more cerise-coloured petals. The other one is the small-flowered cranesbill (*G. pusillum*), whose leaves fall somewhere between the other two species in appearance, the flowers similar in colour to the cut-leaved geranium. Dove's-foot cranesbill flowers from April to September, the others from May to August.

How to grow

Height 30cm (12in)
Habitat Meadow land, roadsides and dry banks.
Garden care These are fairly insignificant plants if grown on their own, but are ideal fillers in summer schemes, for instance between bloody cranesbill, pink pansies or contrasting white or blue flowers. Need deadheading regularly.
Propagation Although only small plants, the annual cranesbills produce quite large seeds, which need scarification, or scratching, to aid germination. They are hardy, so can be sown in autumn or spring. Seed is available from specialist nurseries.

◀ **Dove's-foot cranesbill (*Geranium molle*)**

Bellis perennis
Daisy

Description

A S CHILDREN, we enjoy the bright, summery white-petalled flowers of the daisy, born singly on hairy stalks above rosettes of spoon-shaped leaves with thick, flattened stems. Then, ironically, as adults, we spend hours trying to eradicate them from our lawns, only to go to the local garden centre or market and buy cultivated varieties of them to edge our garden borders and window boxes in the spring. The native plant can flower all year, but mainly from April to July. The cultivated varieties of it – some pink, some red, some semi-double, others fully double with the yellow centre completely hidden in a pompom of bright petals – are grown as biennials and flower over the same period.

How to grow

Height 7cm (2¾in)
Habitat Short grassland.
Garden care Ideal for the rockery, border edging and container planting in sun or partial shade.
Propagation Sow seed in early summer and overwinter plants for flowering the following year, or lift and divide in spring. Commercial varieties are widely available in spring as plants. Seed of the native species is available from specialist nurseries or plants can be transplanted from most lawns.

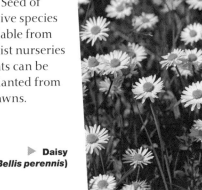

▶ **Daisy**
(*Bellis perennis*)

Viola tricolor
Heartsease

Description

T HIS EXTREMELY variable little flower is the parent of all those hundreds of different pansies, which are sold all through the year. It has small flowers, maybe 2.5cm (1in) or so tall by 2cm (¾in) across, sometimes all yellow, sometimes yellow and white or yellow and purple, sometimes with stripes radiating from the centre, sometimes not. It is a sprawling plant with fairly lax stems and mid-green leaves often held in bunches from the stem. The lower leaves are rounded and heart-shaped with toothed edges, while the upper leaves are longer, narrowing towards the base. The plant flowers from April to September. There is a very similar species, the field pansy (*V. arvensis*), the flowers of which tend to be mainly white or pale yellow.

How to grow

Height 5–45cm (2–18in)
Habitat Field edges, scrubland, meadows and rocky places and can thrive in sun or light shade.
Garden care Deadheading will keep the plants flowering through the season. Cut back stems when they get straggly and at the end of flowering. Water when the weather is hot.
Propagation Seed and plants are available from specialist nurseries. If cultivated pansies are allowed to seed, some will revert to the species type. Cuttings can be taken in summer and potted up with a plastic bag over the top to retain moisture.

◀ **Heartsease**
(*Viola tricolor*)

Umbilicus rupestris
Navelwort

Description

ALSO KNOWN as wall pennywort, this shade-tolerant perennial is often found on walls and rocky banks, especially where there is a source of moisture. Its roots can penetrate deep into the cracks of a wall to draw out any water for the smooth, fleshy round leaves and short spike of drooping creamy-green flowers. The leaves are about the size of an old penny (giving it its alternate name) with a dimple in the centre where the stem attaches to the underside. They are often quite pale. The flower stem is reddish, the flowers appearing from June to August. After setting seed, the plant turns to a reddish-brown colour, then dies back until the following spring.

How to grow

Height 30cm (12in)
Habitat Old walls, steep banks and cliff faces, especially in or on the edge of woodland. Tolerates sun or shade.
Garden care Surprisingly hardy plant. Once established, needs little maintenance. Simply tidy up dead leaves and flower stems in autumn.
Propagation Seed and plants are available from nurseries and some garden centres. Planting in the cracks of a rock face is best done with a pinch of seeds. Plants can be placed in more easily worked sites. Water in well after planting.

► **Navelwort
(Umbilicus rupestris)**

Pulsatilla vulgaris
Pasque flower

Description

NAMED AFTER the Norman French word for Easter, which is when it flowers, this is one of our most beautiful native flowers and now a rare one in the wild. It is widely used in gardens, both the natural purplish-mauve colour and the cultivated white and red forms. Much-divided, soft, feathery grey leaves form a basal rosette, which is almost evergreen, dying back in late summer or autumn to reappear in winter. From the centre of this arise hairy stems, each with a single bud at its apex, above a whorl of leaves. When the cup-shaped flowers open, from March to May, they contain a large boss of bright-yellow stamens, surrounding a dark-purple stigma. Later, the flowers are replaced by hairy seed heads. It is an essential for any garden, especially one on neutral or limy soil.

How to grow

Height 10–30cm (4–12in)
Habitat Dry grassland on alkaline soils, such as the South Downs of southern England.
Garden care Ensure that the soil is not acidic before attempting to grow this plant. Place in a sunny spot. Tidy up the leaves when they die back and cut back most of the seed heads if you do not require the seed.
Propagation Plants and seed are available from garden centres and nurseries. Seed can be saved from plants in the garden and sown in pots in summer.

◄ **Pasque flower
(Pulsatilla vulgaris)**

Succisa pratensis
Scabious (devil's bit)

Description

THE SCABIOUS family are close relatives of the teasels, but on a very different scale. This dainty little plant has blue or bluish-purple flower heads about 2cm (¾in) across, in the form of a tight ball with a flattened base, each on the end of its own slim, softly hairy stem. The slender leaves are in a rough basal rosette, with sometimes a few up the stalks. The scabious family take their name from the skin disease scabies, which the juice of the field scabious was used to cure. And why devil's bit? The plant got its name because the thick root ends abruptly, rather than tapering away, so it was suggested that the devil had come up from beneath the surface of the earth and bitten it off for its curative properties.

There is a similar species, the small scabious (*Scabiosa columbaria*), which usually grows on lime-rich soil and has paler blue flowers, more like a miniature scabious flower in form, and divided leaves as opposed to the entire ones of the devil's bit. The two plants are much the same size, though the devil's bit can grow taller. Both enjoy full sun and both flower from July to October. A third, totally unrelated species, the sheep's-bit (p29) looks very similar, though there are several pale-blue flowers to a stem. It flowers from June to August and is a member of the bellflower family.

How to grow

Height Up to 60cm (24in), but more usually reaches 15–22cm (6–9in). In exposed situations, it will flower at just 7.5cm (3in).

Habitat Very adaptable, being happy in fens, meadows, hedgerows and poor grassland. The small scabious prefers an acid-free soil and the sheep's-bit can tolerate some shade: it can sometimes be found in dry pine woods.

Garden care Choose from the three plants according to your conditions or the preferred colour if giving them a dry, sunny site with neutral soil, where they will all thrive. Their delicate looks are misleading and little care will be required.

Propagation Seed and plants are available from specialist nurseries and sometimes from larger garden centres. Seed is easily collected in autumn and is best sown fresh in pots or seed trays. Bellflowers, including the sheep's-bit, need a period of cold before they will germinate, so do not expect germination until spring for this species.

▶ **Devil's bit scabious (*Succisa pratensis*)**

Cochlearia officinalis
Scurvy grass

Description

A SINGULARLY UNATTRACTIVE name for this attractive plant which is by no means related to the grasses, though the leaves contain high levels of vitamin C and therefore do cure scurvy. Scurvy grass is a very variable plant with heart-shaped, mid-green leaves, the veins often highlighted in dark brown. It forms mounds of thick-stemmed foliage in a wide range of habitats. From mid spring onwards, right through to September, the foliage is fairly well hidden by a profusion of four-petalled white flowers about 1cm (½in) across, which are followed by pea-sized seed pods.

How to grow

Height Up to 45cm (18in)
Habitat Very adaptable, as scurvy grass will grow in salt marshes, beside mountain streams or on dry roadside banks as well as on cliffs and walls.
Garden care Deadheading will maintain the intensity of the flowering through the summer. A liquid feed every two or three weeks in the flowering season will do it good.
Propagation Seed is available from specialist nurseries. This should be sown in pots or where it is to flower in summer and kept moist to aid germination. Seed can be saved from existing plants in the garden. The plant can be lifted and divided every two or three years in spring or autumn.

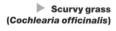

▶ **Scurvy grass (Cochlearia officinalis)**

Potentilla anserina
Silverweed

Description

T HIS LOW–GROWING, creeping perennial brings its silvery leaves, which are sub-divided into deeply toothed leaflets and up to 20cm (8in) long, to almost anywhere its seed will carry to. Its bright yellow flowers can be up to almost 2.5cm (1in) across, the five petals slightly darker towards the centre of the flower. They are carried individually on long stalks from late May until August or even September. Silverweed has over-ground runners up to 45cm (18in) long, which root at the nodes producing new plants. It looks brilliant in bright sunshine, especially when contrasted with something dark like a heather, or blue like a speedwell. An excellent plant for the rockery or border edge.

How to grow

Height 15cm (6in)
Habitat Just about anywhere, from flood meadows and lake shores to dry clay or even shingle beaches. Also found in woodland and common on road verges.
Garden care Water in well when planting. Deadhead regularly to prolong flowering and cut back runners to confine the plant.
Propagation Seed and plants are available from some nurseries. Seed can be saved and sown in late summer. Runners can be allowed to root, then the new plants cut away and transplanted.

▼ **Silverweed (Potentilla anserina)**

Veronica chamaedrys
Speedwell (germander)

Description

ONE OF 18 species of speedwell that grow wild in the United Kingdom, not all of which are native. The bright blue flowers of this pretty perennial are borne on short spikes up to 20cm (8in) long, depending on growing conditions. Often the spikes are much shorter when it has little competition for light. The leaves are broad, hairy and toothed, the stems having two opposite rows of hairs. The flowers, borne from April to July, have a white 'eye', which gives the plant its other common name of 'bird's-eye', as well as two long, white stamens. Often the uppermost of the four petals has dark blue veins radiating from its base.

Wood speedwell (*V. montana*) is similar, but the leaves are stalked and the flowers smaller and more lilac in colour, with the stem hairy all round. Common speedwell (*V. officinalis*) is hairy like the wood speedwell, but with unstalked leaves like the germander and lilac flowers. There are also a number of annual species, including Buxbaum's speedwell (*V. persica*), which has shiny green leaves and bright blue flowers for most of the year. Even wetlands have their own speedwells, the longer-leaved marsh speedwell and water speedwell, discussed in the relevant chapters of this book. Probably the most commonly seen wild form, however, is not a native, having been introduced from the Caucasus. This is the slender speedwell (*V. filiformis*), which has long, creeping stems with small, rounded leaves and bright blue flowers, and is a common weed of lawns throughout the country. There are numerous tall garden veronicas, bred from foreign species for the mixed border.

How to grow

Height Up to 20cm (8in) in a shaded or densely planted situation; more usually 7.5–10cm (3–4in)
Habitat Found in hedgerows and grassland. Likes the sun, so makes a very good rockery or border edging plant.
Garden care Avoid ericaceous soils. Deadhead regularly to extend the flowering season. Clip back stems to keep the plant where it is required.
Propagation Plants and seed are available from nurseries. Seed can be sown throughout the warmer months in pots or trays of good compost. The plants will spread by creeping stems, which root if given the opportunity. Once established, these can be separated from the parent and replanted where required.

▼ **Germander speedwell (*Veronica chamaedrys*)**

Sedum acre
Stonecrop (biting)

Description

ONE OF three yellow–flowered stonecrops native to Britain, this pretty mat–forming perennial is also known as 'wall pepper' for its sharp taste. Its prostrate stems are much–branched and tightly covered with tiny, fleshy oval leaves with a flat upper surface. The flowers are 1cm (½in) across, bright–yellow five–petalled stars, which are borne in small bunches at or near the tips of the stems. The plant will root in the driest of places, even halfway up the side of a stone wall, and can be invasive. It will spread eventually to about 60cm (24in) across and is covered in flowers from early June until late August, especially if you deadhead it regularly. This is a very valuable plant for those places where little else will be tough enough to grow.

How to grow

Height About 10cm (4in); spread up to 60cm (24in)
Habitat Dry banks, walls and dunes in full sun.
Garden care If required in awkward places, like a wall, plant seeds in a tiny bit of soil, rather than compost, and water well with a spray. It should germinate quickly. In easier places, plants can be just tucked in and watered.
Propagation Seed and plants are available from nurseries and some garden centres. Cuttings can be taken in summer from existing plants and rooted in pots of coarse compost.

Sedum anglicum
Stonecrop (English)

Description

ONE OF two white–flowered species of stonecrop native to Britain, this one is found only in the west and is distinguished from its more widespread relative, the white stonecrop (*S. album*), by having smaller leaves that hold tight to the stem and flower stems that are branched only once rather than several times. Found naturally growing over rocks in sunny positions, these plants are ideally suited to the rockery situation or to walls. Their five–petalled flowers are held in profusion above the succulent leaves from May to August in even the driest conditions.

How to grow

Height The English stonecrop grows to just 7.5cm (3in); the white stonecrop up to 22cm (9in).
Habitat Rocks, cliffs and dry places, but will thrive in better conditions if lack of competition allows.
Garden care The main task with these plants is pruning, as they will spread vigorously if allowed. There is a yellow–flowered and grey–leaved variety of the white stonecrop called 'Coral Carpet' which is available from garden centres and spreads to only 22cm (9in) across – this is much more manageable in a small rockery.
Propagation Plants and seeds are available from nurseries and garden centres. Cuttings can be taken and rooted in sandy compost in the growing season.

▼ **English stonecrop (*Sedum anglicum*)**

▶ **Biting stonecrop (*Sedum acre*)**

Fragaria vesca
Strawberry (wild)

Description

WITH FIVE-PETALLED white flowers 1–2.5cm (½–1in) across from April right through the summer, the wild strawberry is a pretty plant for the shady side of a rockery, even without the fruit. These are much smaller than the cultivated varieties, which originate in America, but very sweet, with prominent pips. The trilobed leaves are mid green, with bold veining and toothed edges. The strawberry was named for the habit of placing straw beneath the berries to keep the dirt off them in wet weather.

How to grow

Height Up to 30cm (12in), but often half that
Habitat Hedges, woods and scrubland, often, but not always, in shade.
Garden care Ensure the crowns are planted exactly at soil level. Picking the fruit is good for the plant, as well as making it produce more, for we tend to pick it before the seeds are actually ripe. Cut back or pot up runners. Look out for viral disease and, if found, destroy the plant. There is also a beetle that attacks the roots. If this occurs, then dig out and discard the surrounding soil.
Propagation Plants and seed are available from nurseries and garden centres. Small plants formed on runners can be potted up, then cut free when rooted, or fruit can be picked when over-ripe and pressed on to the surface of a pot of compost so that the seed will germinate in the autumn.

▶ **Wild strawberry (*Fragaria vesca*)**

Armeria maritima
Thrift

Description

ALSO KNOWN as 'sea pink', this neat little perennial has grassy leaves and pink pompoms of flowers about 2.5cm (1in) across. It is one of the staples of any rock garden, as well as brightening the cliffs and shores of our coastline. The hummocks of foliage are evergreen, spreading to over 30cm (12in) across. The flowers are borne on bare, slender stems up to 15cm (6in) long, in profusion from May to September. Usually they are pink, but there is a white variety seen occasionally in the wild and also available in some garden centres and one with variegated leaves.

How to grow

Height Occasionally up to 30cm (12in), but more usually half that
Habitat Found on cliff tops, mountains, salt marshes and shingle. Very well adapted to conserve moisture, but it does not like shade.
Garden care Water in well when planting, deadhead to extend the flowering season and clip back the main stems to confine it if necessary.
Propagation Plants are readily available from nurseries, garden centres and market stalls. Seed is also available from some nurseries. The creeping stems can be cut back and the cuttings trimmed and potted up in gritty compost to root in a few weeks.

◀ **Thrift (*Armeria maritima*)**

Thymus praecox
Thyme (wild)

Description

ONE OF several species of wild thyme that grow in Britain, this carpeting aromatic sub–shrub thrives on dry banks, rocky places and even sand dunes. It is tolerant of acid or limy soils and enjoys a sunny aspect. Thymes are invaluable in the kitchen for their aromatic leaves as well as in the garden, where their pinkish flowers will brighten a warm spot in the height of summer. Wild thyme flowers mainly in early summer, but with regular deadheading will continue through until early autumn. It is a low, spreading plant, achieving a width of anything up to 60cm (24in), but a height of only 10cm (4in) when in flower. The prostrate main stems send up vertical flowering stalks with the characteristic round to oval flower heads at the tops.

Similar species include common thyme (*T. vulgaris*), a shrubby evergreen with dark green leaves, which grows to 30cm (12in) high and flowers throughout the summer. Also broad–leaved or large thyme (*T. pulegioides*), which again has dark green leaves and flowers right through the summer, but grows to only 7.5–10cm (3–4in).

Breckland thyme (*T. serpyllum*) is rare in the wild, but is the variety most taken to by gardeners. This has narrow, dark green leaves, darker flowers than the others, a low, creeping habit and again flowers from June to September.

How to grow

Height 10cm (4in) when in flower
Habitat Dry, sunny places such as grassy banks, limestone pavements, scree and sand dunes.
Garden care Water in well when planting. Deadhead regularly to prolong the flowering period. Prune to maintain shape and size.
Propagation Thymes, both native and imported, are commonly available in garden centres and nurseries, especially in early summer. Almost all are evergreen and can be planted from the pot whenever the weather is not too cold, though they are best planted in summer. Softwood cuttings can be taken during the warmer months and potted in gritty compost to root in a sheltered area.

▼ **Wild thyme (*Thymus praecox*)**

Verbena officinalis
Vervain

Description

EXQUISITE LITTLE mauve flowers decorate this relative of the garden verbenas, which were bred from imported American species, from June to September. A plant for the front of the border or rockery, where it can be enjoyed from close up, it has undivided, toothed leaves at the base and near the tops of the branching, squarish stems. Between these two areas, the leaves are finely divided, giving a ferny effect. There are coarse hairs on the angles of the stems of this constituent of salves and medicines since at least the days of the Celts, from whom the name comes. The small flowers are borne in long, slender spikes, not all the flowers on a spike being out at the same time.

How to grow

Height 30–60cm (12–24in)
Habitat Dry, stony places such as walls, scree slopes and footpath edges as well as meadows and will thrive in full sun or partial shade.
Garden care Water in well when planting, but should not need further watering. Remove flowering spike when it is finished to encourage more spikes and cut back hard at the end of the season.
Propagation Plants and seed are available from nurseries. Seed can be saved from existing plants in the garden and sown in late summer in pots or trays outside or where it is to flower.

▶ **Vervain**
(***Verbena officinalis***)

Draba aizoides
Whitlow-grass (yellow)

Description

RARELY HAS there been a more inappropriate–sounding Latin name given to a plant than *Draba* for this brilliant little gem. Confined in the wild to one small area in south Wales, it is now becoming popular in gardens. The narrow, dark green evergreen leaves are just 2.5cm (1in) or so long and fringed with bristles, growing in little tufts. The stems are leafless, with bunches of bright, starry little sulphur–yellow flowers at the tops which have rounded petals and many stamens. It begins to flower early, sometimes in March, and continues sporadically until August, the flowers being around 1.5cm (½in) across.

How to grow

Height Up to about 10cm (4in)
Habitat Likes open grassland, scree slopes and rocky areas, often on alkaline soils. Not a moisture–lover, but does need plenty of sun.
Garden care Place this perennial where it can be seen and enjoyed from close–up, as it will stay small. Deadhead to extend the flowering season and allow the plant to grow rather than set seeds.
Propagation Plants and seed are available from good garden centres and nurseries. Seed can be saved from existing plants in the garden or the little leaf rosettes can be cut away and planted up as cuttings in pots in summer.

◀ **Yellow whitlow-grass**
(***Draba aizoides***)

Although wildflower meadows are rare now and becoming rarer with modern farm practices, they are still around and once seen, they will truly inspire. There is nothing like the blaze of colour you can get in a good meadow to bring out the wish for such a brilliant display in your garden. The plants included here will provide colour from April right through the summer and autumn, and if you use grasses and teasel as well, you will have interest and form through the winter too.

Meadow plants

Growing meadow plants

A LTHOUGH VERY few people have a garden big enough to accommodate a meadow, a small area of meadow plants can look very effective. Even a 1m by 3m (3ft by 9ft) brick–sided raised bed filled to overflowing with meadow plants can look quite spectacular and, contrary to popular belief, can be colourful far beyond the height of summer.

Starting your patch

I F YOU want to create a meadow patch, clearing the ground thoroughly first gives the best results. Remove all traces of perennial weeds – you can even leave it for a season and use weedkiller, or remove by hand the young weeds that will almost inevitably emerge – then sow

with a seed mix of meadow grass and annual wild flowers. This will include cornflowers (p60), corn marigolds (p65), poppies (p68), corn chamomile (p60), and perhaps corn cockle though this is not native to Britain.

The seed should be raked in, watered and netted if possible to keep off birds and other seed–stealers. If netting is not possible, do not worry: the sowing rates on seed packs always allow a little surplus, and any significant gaps can be filled in later.

When germination has taken place, leave the patch for a further two to three weeks before walking on it, to allow the new plants to establish. At this point, you can re–sow in any thin areas and insert plug plants of the meadow perennials such as buttercup (p58), ox–eye daisy (p66), cranesbill (p61), meadow clary (*Salvia pratensis*), cowslip (p61) and sainfoin (p70).

▼ **Meadow plan with red-themed planting.**

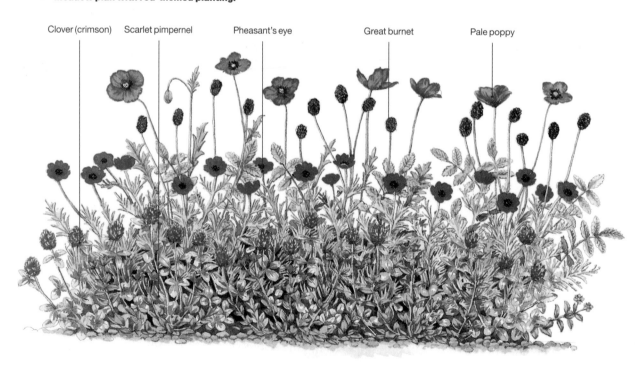

Clover (crimson)   Scarlet pimpernel   Pheasant's eye   Great burnet   Pale poppy

Mowing and clipping

D O NOT cut new grass for at least six weeks after sowing, and then only lightly to thicken it up and encourage branching of the stems. Do not worry if you mow the tops off flowering plants: they are adapted to this, and will simply flower a little later and be a little shorter. Mature flowering heights are specified for the different plants, but many will flower at much shorter heights if they have been cut down early in the year. Usually 90cm (36in), the mallows, for instance, will flower at just 10cm (4in) high at the edge of a lawn. Another option is to sow the seeds in autumn or early spring (they are hardy after all), wait for them to reach about 20cm (8in) tall, then trim them down to roughly half that height with shears. This will

▼ **Plan for a meadow in early summer.**

Sowing annuals

Meadow annuals tend to dislike root disturbance, so they are best sown where they are to flower, and sown twice as thickly as you would other plants.

do two things. Firstly, it will make them into bushier, stronger plants with more flowers and secondly, it will make them flower slightly later than they would have otherwise. This can be done two or even three times, each time making them bushier, stronger and more floriferous – and shorter by the time they flower – and each time making them later to flower. In this way, you can extend the flowering season considerably. Deadheading will add even further to this.

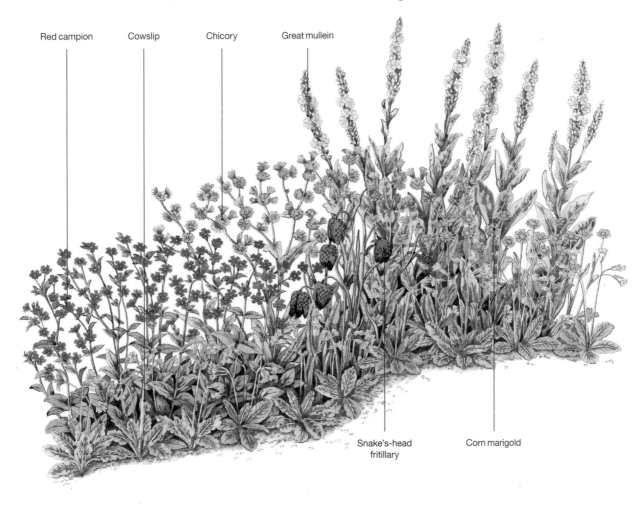

Red campion   Cowslip   Chicory   Great mullein

Snake's-head fritillary   Corn marigold

Meadow maintenance

IN FUTURE years, mow the meadow only after flowering has finished. This will encourage a second flush of flowers on some plants. After this, the meadow can be mown again and through the autumn. An early spring mowing is useful, unless any spring–flowering bulbs such as daffodil (p141) or snake's–head fritillaries (*Fritillaria meleagris*) have been included.

Although most meadow plants are annuals, they seed prolifically and should replace themselves each year with or without your help as long as you don't deadhead or mow them until after they have set seed in late summer. If they appear in the wrong place, all you need do is pull or dig them up. If you are careful with the roots, then you can even replant them where you want them.

Flowering additions to lawns

A more formal lawn created with regular lawn seed or turf can have flowering additions, as long as they flower in spring before the lawn needs mowing too much. Patches of daffodils (p141) are now a common sight in lawn grass. The disadvantage of this is that the leaves should be left on the plants until at least six weeks after flowering. During this time the grass between them cannot be mown, and this increases the likelihood that weeds will take hold. Patches of daisies (p41) or cowslips (p61) can be equally effective in the lawn. They look very pretty in spring and can be mown over later. Surplus plants can be dug out as plugs and placed in the border, or put in pots to be given away or sold. The patches can be kept in bounds by using a weed and feed mix on the surrounding lawn.

▼ **Plan for a meadow mixed with grasses in early summer.**

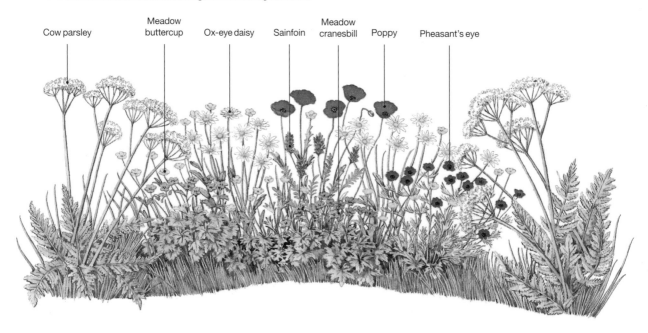

Cow parsley   Meadow buttercup   Ox-eye daisy   Sainfoin   Meadow cranesbill   Poppy   Pheasant's eye

▲ **Red campion and Queen Anne's lace combine for a two-tone effect through late spring and early summer.**

Soil and position

THERE IS a commonly held myth that meadow plants need poor soil in order to give of their best. This originates with the observation that they grow in close competition with and physically supported by other plants and grasses, but it is nevertheless not true. What is true is that the wild forms of many meadow plants have evolved to compete for both light and nutrients and to rely on the support of their neighbours so will look lax and poorly if grown as you would border annuals.

Plant choices

THERE ARE two basic types of meadows, populated by two different groups of plants. Wet meadows have plants that would be equally at home in a marshy area, whereas dry-meadow plants would be just as happy in a rockery. There is, of course, some overlap between the two groups. Also, early-mown or grazed meadows will often have a different flora from those mown later. The shorter grass areas could hold cowslips (p61), orchids, milk vetch (*Astragalus boeticus*), bird's-foot trefoil (p81), and hare's foot clover (*Trifolium arvense*) whereas the later-mown, longer grass might contain meadow clary, chicory (*Cichorium intybus*), meadow vetchling (p170) as well as cornflowers (p60), corn marigolds (p65)

and field poppies (p68). And for contrast among all this vivid brightness, it is difficult to beat the upright reddish spires of sheep's sorrel (*Rumex acetosella*) or the waving dark maroon blobs of the round-headed leek (*Allium sphaerocephalum*).

Planting need not create a kaleidoscope of colours. A more limited palette can look equally effective. The pale pink of musk mallow (p24), for example, combines very well with the rich yellow of hawk's beard (p64) or St John's wort (p30) in a two-colour combination. In a red garden, field poppies and knapweed (p65), perhaps with sainfoin (p70) or red campion (p59), look great. Buttercups (p58) and ox-eye daisies (p66) make a lovely combination, or you can go for the multi-coloured option and mix corn marigolds with cornflowers, poppies, ox-eye daisies and Queen Anne's Lace (p69) for a summer extravaganza.

It can also be effective to combine meadow plants with decorative grasses, perhaps in drifts through each other rather than in a haphazard, meadow-like mixture.

Grasses
No meadow would be complete without its grasses. Apart from their obvious use in the lawn, grasses are highly decorative plants for a number of situations in the garden, adding their particular form and texture to beds and borders, in sun or shade as well as in the marshy places or even in the pond.

Galium verum
Bedstraw (lady's)

Description

THIS SWEET–SMELLING perennial meadow flower was once dried and used to line mattresses. Its stems are up to 60cm (24in) tall but fairly weak and fine, needing the support of surrounding plants. Its long, dense panicles of bright yellow flowers look excellent with goldenrod (*Solidago virgaurea*), mullein (p66) and wild parsnip (p67), or for a mixed-colour arrangement red valerian (*Centranthus ruber*), various bellflowers, cornflowers and poppies will make an attractive combination from early June through to September. The bedstraws are a varied family, including the similar but taller and white-flowered hedge bedstraw (*G. mollugo*), sweet woodruff (p152) and the less welcome goose grass (*G. aparine*).

How to grow

Height Up to 60cm (24in)
Habitat Meadows, dry grassland and open woods, where it can find a sunny position.
Garden care Deadhead to extend the flowering season. They are best planted close to the house, so that the sweet scented flowers can be enjoyed through the summer.
Propagation Seed and plants are available from specialist nurseries throughout Britain. Seed should be sown in late summer or early autumn in pots or trays. Young plants can be planted out as soon as they are large enough to handle or kept in pots until springtime.

▶ **Lady's bedstraw
(*Galium verum*)**

Ranunculus sp.
Buttercup

Description

SEVERAL SPECIES of buttercup are native to Britain. Probably the most useful of these for the garden is the bulbous buttercup (*R. bulbosa*). This is the classic, golden-yellow, cup-shaped flower of childhood games. The flowers are about 2.5cm (1in) across with the sepals turned back along the furrowed stem. This plant enjoys drier conditions than the other buttercups and prefers lime-rich soil. Of its close relatives, the creeping buttercup (*R. repens*) is not recommended for garden use as it is too invasive. The leaves of this one are broader and the sepals stay tight to the backs of the petals. Another commonly found species is the meadow buttercup (*R. acris*). This is a much-branched plant, taller than the others at 1m (3ft), and its stems are not ridged like those of the others. The flower is cup-shaped, but the sepals lie close to the petals. The bulbous buttercup flowers in May and June, the others from May to September.

How to grow

Height Up to 40cm (16in) for bulbous buttercups.
Habitat Bulbous buttercups prefer dry pasture and lime rich soil. The others like moist soil.
Garden care All species are meadowland plants so like a restricted root-run and some support. Plant close together for a bold statement or close to other plants for a more natural effect.
Propagation Seeds are available from specialist wildflower nurseries.

◀ **Buttercup
(*Ranunculus sp.*)**

Silene
Campion (red and white)

Description

THESE DIOECIOUS perennials – there are separate male and female plants – can be found in hedgerows, ditches, field margins and meadows. The flowers are about 2.5cm (1in) across and are borne on branching stems up to 75cm (30in) high, rising from an evergreen rosette of oval hairy leaves. Leaves further up the stems are narrower, with shorter stalks. They begin to flower in late spring and will continue through to early autumn. The petals are deeply notched at the tips and attractive to butterflies.

Red campion (*S. dioica*) will thrive anywhere as long as it gets some shade for at least part of the day. The wild form is a very beautiful plant, but needs cutting down after flowering unless the seed is required. There is also a pretty double version with larger flowers called 'Flore Pleno', and a dwarf variety called 'Minnikin'.

White campion (*S. alba*) has larger, fuller flowers and prefers more open ground. It grows in the sunny edges of arable fields and on waste ground, as well as close to the red campion in hedgerow bottoms, where the two occasionally hybridize to give a pale–pink offspring. The white campion flowers are subtly scented, especially in the evening. It is taller than the bladder campion (*S. vulgaris*) for which it is occasionally confused at a distance.

How to grow

Height Up to 1m (3ft)

Habitat Red campion is found on the shady side of hedgerows, ditches, woodlands and tall herb communities, usually on neutral to alkaline soils. White campion tends towards the more open ground of meadows, field margins, hedgerows and dry banks.

Garden care Water in well when planting, which is best done in autumn or early spring. Deadhead to keep the flower display going through the season and cut the plants down to the basal rosette of stalked oval leaves in late autumn.

Propagation Seed and plants are available from nurseries and the cultivated forms can be found as plants in some garden centres. Seed can be saved and sown in pots or where it is to flower, in autumn or spring. Plants can be divided every three years. Cuttings can be taken in summer and potted in plastic bags to root in a few weeks outside or in the cold frame.

▼ **(Left to right) White campion (*Silene alba*) and red campion (*Silene dioica*)**

Anthemis arvensis
Chamomile (corn)

Description

A HAIRY PLANT with finely cut leaves, sometimes hairy underneath. It has neat daisy flowers 2–4cm (¾–1½in) across, borne in profusion over the plant from May to July and pleasantly, though not strongly, fragrant. Not to be confused with its close relative, also native, the stinking chamomile (*A. cotula*), which smells rank, is almost hairless and flowers from July to September. There is a third native chamomile: the lawn variety (*A. nobilis*), which is a perennial. This also has white daisy–type flowers, but is much stronger and sweeter smelling and flowers from June to August.

How to grow

Height 30–45cm (12–18in)
Habitat Arable and wasteland, it prefers lime–rich soil and full sun.
Garden care Deadheading is important as without it there will be one good flush then no more.
Propagation Lawn chamomile is widely available from nurseries and garden centres. Corn chamomile has to come from the more specialized places. Seed can be sown in autumn or spring, in trays or where it is to flower. Pruning the plants hard immediately after flowering, without allowing them to set seed, can sometimes make them last into the following year.

▶ **Corn chamomile (*Anthemis arvensis*)**

Centaurea cyanus
Cornflower (annual)

Description

T HIS NATURALLY blue–flowered annual has been through a lot of changes in the past 40 years or so. Once common as a weed of arable land, it is now rare in the wild, but very common in gardens. It has been bred to give dwarf varieties as well as the full–sized ones and white, pink, or red–flowered types. Flowering from June to September, cornflowers give good value for money and the seeds are hardy, lasting for years if kept dry. It's a deservedly popular, slim grey-leaved plant for most types of garden.

How to grow

Height Up to 1m (3ft)
Habitat Naturally a plant of dry grassland and arable fields, it can thrive in any well–drained soil, in sun or partial shade.
Garden care Water in well when planting pot-grown plants. Deadhead regularly for a good, continuous show of flowers and pull out when flowering is finished.
Propagation Seed is available from garden centres and nurseries. It can be sown in autumn or spring, as this is a hardy annual. Autumn–sown plants tends to be stronger and bushier. Seed can be saved from your own plants but will not necessarily be true to variety.

◀ **Annual cornflower (*Centaurea cyanus*)**

Primula veris
Cowslip

Description

THIS LOVELY spring flower is politely named for what it tends to grow best in – cow dung. Its small yellow flowers with long yellowy green tubular calices nod gently in bunches at the tops of long, slender stems. The stems rise up from a basal rosette of crinkled, softly hairy, mid green, tongue-like leaves. The flowers smell faintly of apricots. Its other close relative which is native to Britain is the oxlip (*P. elatior*), now a rare plant in the wild. This has larger, paler, scentless flowers and is a woodland flower, blooming from March to May. The cowslip flowers at the same time.

How to grow

Height Flowering stems up to 25cm (10in)
Habitat Favours old grassland, including roadsides and orchards. Can tolerate sun or shade but is not a lover of excess moisture.
Garden care Deadhead when the flowering stem has finished and the plant may well put up another and even another. A late one can be left on the plant if seed is required. Lift and divide clumps every couple of years.
Propagation Plants and seed are available from nurseries and some garden centres. The seed needs to be sown fresh and will take until at least the next spring to germinate, as it needs the cold of winter to break its dormancy. Divide and replant clumps before flowering in spring.

▶ **Cowslip**
(*Primula veris*)

Geranium pratense
Cranesbill (meadow)

Description

THE MEADOW cranesbill is a popular garden plant, its bright-blue flowers decorating the mixed border as well as its natural habitat from June to September. The dark green leaves are deeply divided and sub-divided, normally in seven lobes coming from a central point where the stalk joins. The blue flowers are five-petalled cups about 2.5cm (1in) across, sometimes with black centres. They are held on branching stems above the leaves. There is an even more floriferous variety called 'Johnson's Blue' and a very handsome white one, 'Alba'. The wood cranesbill (*G. sylvaticum*) also has blue flowers, though they are smaller and more mauve than the meadow cranesbill and the leaves are smaller and less divided.

How to grow

Height Up to 60cm (24in), but often half that
Habitat Damp meadows, woodland and roadsides, in sun or light shade.
Garden care Water in well when planting. Deadhead regularly and tidy up old leaves at the end of the growing season and you will be rewarded with a display for years.
Propagation Seed and plants are widely available from garden centres and nurseries. The wood cranesbill, along with some of the other less-used species, can be found in specialist nurseries.

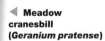
◀ **Meadow cranesbill**
(*Geranium pratense*)

Grasses

THERE ARE three types of plants growing wild in Britain, which are, or can be mistaken for, grasses. The sedges are usually plants of wetland habitat. Most have several groups of flowers along the stem, which is triangular in section, the leaves having a strong mid–rib on their underside. The rushes have tubular stems, often with a pithy centre, and the leaves tend to be rolled lengthwise so that they are round in section and there is no upper or lower surface. The true grasses have jointed stems, often with a leaf arising from the joint. The stems are round and the leaves usually flat, the base of the leaf often wrapped around the stem from where it emerges. So too are those of the reeds, which are simply large grasses, usually of wetland habitats. There are over 100 species of grasses, sedges and reeds native to the UK, many with potential as attractive meadow plants.

Meadow grass (wood)
(Poa nemoralis)

A LOOSELY TUFTED perennial, this common grass is tolerant of sun or shade, growing in parks and meadows as well as the woods from which it draws its name. It is a hairless plant with thin, pale green leaves and a loose, finely branched flower spike that is somewhat nodding until flowering is over, when it becomes erect. A very pretty and adaptable little grass, usually growing to about 30cm (12in) high, though it can be considerably taller in a shady situation. It dies back in winter, when the tufts can be cut short in preparation for next year's growth.

Dog's-tail (crested)
(Cymosurus cristatus)

TUFTED PERENNIAL up to 75cm (30in) tall with erect, smooth stalks and leaves that sometimes curl lengthwise. Flower panicles are dense, spike–like and greenish, with the spikelets arranged in two rows up the stem. These are quite one-sided, the stem itself angling in a wavy fashion from one pair of spikelets to the next and back again. Crested dog's-tail flowers in June and July, growing naturally in meadows and on the sides of roads and paths, generally in sunny situations. The plant persists long into the autumn, when it is more noticeable in the wild, for it is too tough to be grazed by animals.

▼ Wood meadow grass (*Poa nemoralis*)

▼ Crested dog's-tail (*Cymosurus cristatus*)

Feather grass (common)
(*Stipa pennata*)

ALTHOUGH SEEN in the photograph growing next to a pool near Oxford, England on the kind of dry, grassy, sunny bank it likes, feather grass was actually introduced from Europe because of its highly decorative appearance. It is a perennial, growing to a little over 60cm (24in) tall. The bristly leaves are a greyish green in colour, the heads and hairs on them silvery in the sunshine. Shown here in May, just before the true inflorescences appear, when they emerge they will be long and feathery, waving and curling in the breeze. This grass is rare in the wild in Britain but very worthwhile in the garden. It can be found in nurseries and some garden centres.

Wild oat (common)
(*Avena fatua*)

THE LOOSE, drooping panicles of flower and later seed of this useful annual nod in the breeze from April onwards, drying on the stem if left, to give a golden haze to the border in winter and readily seed itself for the following year. The jointed, grass–like stems grow up to 60cm (24in). These and the rough leaves are a light green colour. The long, narrow flowers hang from the tips of fine, branching stems. Looks very elegant when grown with something dark behind or through something shorter and rounded in form, such as the perennial cornflower (*Centaurea montana*) or some of the campanulas. A plant of sunny places on roadsides and waste ground, it needs some moisture, so is best watered in very dry weather.

Quaking grass
(*Briza media*)

THIS PERENNIAL grass forms loose tufts of mid green leaves up to about 15cm (6in) high. From these, in May and through to August, arise tall, very slender flowering stems, pale green turning to straw colour. The stems bear loose, very open panicles of flowers. These are born in heart shaped bunches, each about 0.5cm (¼in) across. These bunches, or spikelets, of flowers are borne widely separated on long, branching stalks and begin life a pale purple colour, with the yellow stamens hanging prominently. The stalks are so fine that the heads wave constantly in the slightest breeze, giving the grass its common name. Looks very decorative on a rockery or somewhere with a dark background.

▼ **Common wild oat (*Avena fatua*)**

▼ **Common feather grass (*Stipa pennata*)**

▼ **Quaking grass (*Briza media*)**

Crepis vesicaria
Hawk's-beard (beaked)

Description

THERE ARE several species of hawk's–beard native to Britain. They are generally 60–100cm (2–3ft) tall and much branched, the yellow flowers resembling those of the dandelion and the hawkweeds. The beaked hawk's–beard is usually about 50cm (20in) tall, branched and wiry, its leaves slender and mostly at the base of the plant, divided like those of the dandelion. Rough hawk's–beard (*C. biennis*) is taller, at about 1m (3ft), its flowers broader, but more ragged–looking, the buds shorter. Smooth hawk's–beard (*C. capillaris*) is about the same height as beaked hawk's–beard, but the flowers are a darker yellow and the buds more rounded. Like rough hawk's–beard, it grows throughout the British Isles, being common in grassland, waste ground and roadsides, flowering in late summer and autumn. Smooth hawk's–beard is the one that may be found on walls and dry slopes. There is also a marsh hawk's–beard, whose flowers are covered with black hairs and which is found in high marshes and bogs. Of them all beaked hawk's–beard is the earliest into flower, blooming in May and continuing all the way through the summer.

How to grow

Height Up to 60cm (24in)
Habitat Meadows and grassland, especially on lime–rich soils.
Garden care Sow directly where it is to flower so that it can establish its crown tight against the soil and will not need any support. Otherwise the wiry stems will fall over if not grown in close association with other plants. Deadhead regularly to keep the strength in the plant.
Propagation Seed is available from specialist wildflower nurseries. Sow seed where it is required to flower in autumn or early spring and water it in well.

▼ **Beaked hawk's beard (*Crepis vesicaria*)**

Centaurea nigra
Knapweed (common)

Description

A HAIRY PLANT, knapweed has elliptical leaves all the way up the stem. The flower head is quite tight and thistle-like, the bud hard and scaled with dark brown bracts. Closely related is the greater knapweed (*C. scabiosa*), which is slightly taller, has large divided basal leaves and small, narrow stem leaves. The flowers are larger, more open and ragged, with long inflorescences around the outside of the head. Both of these flower between June and September.

How to grow

Height Common knapweed grows up to 60cm (24in), greater knapweed up to about 1m (3ft).
Habitat Both are found in meadows, grassland and on footpaths. Common knapweed is sometimes seen on cliffs.
Garden care Like plenty of sun and can take a dryish soil but need a deep root-run. Although they are meadow plants, they are generally able to support themselves without staking.
Propagation Seed and plants can be found in most garden centres.

▼ Common knapweed (*Centaurea nigra*)

Chrysanthemum segetum
Marigold (corn)

Description

B RIGHT YELLOW, daisy-like flowers up to 5cm (2in) across make a bold statement in a summer meadow or border. This upright, branching annual flowers from June to September above smooth, scented, bluish-green, fleshy leaves. A plant that looks spectacular in a group.

How to grow

Height 15–45cm (6–18in), depending on the closeness of planting
Habitat Once a common weed of cornfields, it is now a rare denizen of sunny, preferably sandy, arable land and waste ground, where its seed can lie dormant for several years if undisturbed.
Garden care Provide a site with plenty of sun. A light soil is preferred but not essential. Deadhead regularly until you want to harvest seed towards the end of the flowering season. Cutting back hard before the plant sets seed may make it last another year.
Propagation Seed is available from specialist nurseries but is also easy to collect from your own plants.

▼ Corn marigold (*Chrysanthemum segetum*)

Verbascum thapsus
Mullein (great)

Description

T HE GREAT mullein or common mullein grows as a biennial, having a large rosette of grey, felty leaves in the first year. From these arise tall, usually unbranched flowering stems in the late spring of the second year. These stems have leaves up their lower portions, leading up to a flower spike that can be 1m (3ft) long and dotted with open yellow flowers about 2.5cm (1in) across. The multi–coloured garden cultivars sold in garden centres are bred from two other species, the purple mullein (*V. phoeniceum*), which is not native, and the handsome dark mullein (*V. nigrum*), which is native. Dark mullein grows anything up to 1.2m (4ft) high, with dark stems and dark centres to the yellow flowers.

How to grow

Height Up to 2.1m (7ft)
Habitat Woodland clearings, roadsides, dry banks and scrub. Tolerates chalk and sandy soils. Can take partial shade. Flowers best in poor, dry soil.
Garden care Plant in poor soil and cut down the flowering stem as soon as it has finished in order to keep the plant for another year.
Propagation Available from nurseries and garden centres. Plants will self–seed if allowed to do so. Root cuttings can be taken before planting out in spring and rooted in pots.

▶ **Great mullein (*Verbascum thapsus*)**

Leucanthemum vulgare
Ox-eye daisy

Description

S OMETIMES ALSO listed as *Chrysanthemum leucanthemum*, this branched, woody–based perennial is also commonly known as the moon daisy. It is very variable in height, depending on where it is growing, but commonly provides sheets of white on roadsides, dry banks and meadows from late May and well into August. The large, daisy–like flowers open at the tops of sparsely hairy green stems with leaves similar to those of the garden chrysanthemums. The basal leaves are long–stalked and rounded, the stem leaves unstalked, long and slender, both with coarsely toothed margins.

How to grow

Height 10–60cm (4–24in), depending on density of planting, how sunny and how moist the site is.
Habitat Naturally found in grassland, on dry banks and railway edges as well as open woodland. Prefers neutral to alkaline soils.
Garden care Water plants in well. Deadhead regularly and cut back hard in autumn when flowering has finished. Mulch with organic matter in spring and divide clumps every few years.
Propagation Plants and seed are available from nurseries. In spring, cuttings can be taken and plants can be lifted and divided.

▼ Ox-eye daisy (*Leucanthemum vulgare*)

Pastinaca sativa
Parsnip (wild)

Description

THIS PERENNIAL herb with yellow flowers, has a strong tap-root that was bred to become thicker and more fleshy until it became the parsnip that is grown as a vegetable in our gardens today. The stiff, downy stems arise in early summer, pale and thick, with rough pinnate leaves folding out from them, their broad lobes toothed. The upper leaves are often very small. The hollow, ridged stems are branched and darken with age to a rich green colour. The tiny bright yellow flowers are borne in much-branched flat terminal panicles from July to September. The plant can provide a stately contrast to goldenrod (*Solidago virgaurea*), yellow (p87) or purple (p86) loosestrife, for instance, in the middle or back of a mixed border.

How to grow

Height Up to 1.2m (4ft)
Habitat Grassy slopes, meadows, roadsides and ditches, especially on chalk and limestone soils.
Garden care Ultra-violet light can react with chemicals in the plant to make it irritating to the skin, so gloves are best worn when handling it. The plant should be watered in well, preferably in a deep soil, and not allowed to dry out too much. Deadheading may extend the flowering season.
Propagation Seed is available from some nurseries and should be sown in mid- to late summer in pots or where it is to flower. Pot-grown plants can be planted out in late spring or early summer.

▶ **Wild parsnip (*Pastinaca sativa*)**

Adonis annua
Pheasant's eye

Description

THIS FEATHERY-LEAVED annual is a member of the buttercup family. It bears 4cm (1.5in) wide, cup-shaped red flowers with black centres from May to August, reminiscent of a small cosmos. This is a deservedly popular garden plant with big, starry, daisy-like flowers, growing to about 75cm (30in). The pheasant's eye flowers are borne singly at the tips of the branched stems. The finely cut pinnate leaves are stalkless, providing a smoky haze of bright green as a background to the vivid flowers. There are four species of pheasant's eye, but only two occur in Britain, the second being large pheasant's eye (*A. flammea*), which is very similar, but has a softly hairy stem.

How to grow

Height Up to 30cm (12in)
Habitat Open grassland and arable land in southern England.
Garden care Best sown where it is to flower. Rake the soil lightly after sowing and water, then simply keep weed-free and deadhead as necessary.
Propagation Seed and plants are available from specialist nurseries. Seed can be saved from existing plants, but like other members of the buttercup family it is best sown fresh.

▼ **Pheasant's eye (*Adonis annua*)**

Papaver rhoeas
Poppy (common)

Description

ONE OF only two truly red flowers native to Britain, the other being the pheasant's eye (p67), the common poppy makes a glorious sight when massed in summer meadows or on roadsides. There are four distinct species of poppy, which can be defined by close examination. The others include the long–headed poppy (*P. dubium*), similar to the common poppy, but with long, narrow fruits (this is sometimes found in a very attractive orange form, as well as the usual red). The rough poppy (*P. hybridum*), has a hairy fruit, rounded like that of the common poppy and finally the prickly poppy (*P. argemone*) has a fruit similar in shape to that of the long–headed poppy but hairy, and the petals are smaller, narrower and well separated. Having said all that, the common poppy gives a wonderful show from May to September, the papery flowers displayed above bristly bright green stems and divided, hairy leaves, and the bristly buds nodding gently between the open flowers with their deep, black centres.

How to grow

Height 20–45cm (8–18in), depending on the density of surrounding planting
Habitat Found in cornfields, waste ground, footpaths and roadside verges, especially where the ground has been disturbed – which is a good reason for using a hoe between your plants.
Garden care Frequent deadheading through the summer will ensure a long display of flowers. Leave a few heads to ripen towards the end of the flowering season and hoe between the plants to encourage seed to set.
Propagation Seed is available from nurseries or once you have the plants you can save your own, though it is best sown fresh, where it is to flower.

◀ ▲ **Common poppy**
(*Papaver rhoeas*)

Anthriscus sylvestris
Queen Anne's lace

Description

ALSO KNOWN as cow parsley and keck in different parts of the country, this plant is one of literally dozens that are native to Britain among the parsley family. Several are edible and have parented cultivated vegetables and herbs. Others, like hemlock (*Conium maculatum*), are very poisonous. The difficulty comes in telling some of them apart. Queen Anne's lace is a useful species in the garden purely for decorative reasons. Its fine filigree of dark green leaves beneath delicate white sprays of tiny flowers makes an excellent substitute for gypsophila, both in the border and in the vase. It flowers from April to August, repeatedly if deadheaded regularly.

How to grow

Height Can grow to 1.5m (5ft), but commonly settles for half that, especially in full sun.
Habitat Roadsides, meadows, woodland and scrub. It will grow in sun, shade and dry or damp soils.
Garden care Water in well when planting, but this should not be needed thereafter. Deadhead regularly. Allow a few heads to stay on at the end of the season and set seed for collection. Leave the old plants in the border over winter, as they look decorative in a winter frost.
Propagation Seed is available from specialist nurseries or can be saved from existing plants and sown in pots outside or where the plants are required, preferably in autumn.

▶ **Queen Anne's lace (*Anthriscus sylvestris*)**

Ononis repens
Restharrow (common)

Description

OBTAINING ITS name by binding (or arresting) the harrow, an ancient cultivation tool used after or instead of the plough, this tough-stemmed perennial of the pea family bears showy, pink, pea-like flowers from July until the autumn. It is most commonly found on dry grassland, but will take well to rockeries or walls. This is one of the non–climbing members of the genus, though it will form a tough tangle of stems, well endowed with flowers through the late summer. Its close relative spiny restharrow (*O. spinosa*) is a little taller at 45cm (18in), its flowers are redder and it prefers heavier soils.

How to grow

Height 30cm (12in)
Habitat Both plants are usually found in dry grassland, path edges and waste ground. They grow in most soil types.
Garden care Sunlight is important to these plants. They will be happy in the border or the rockery, but do not let them get too crowded out.
Propagation Seed can be sown in autumn or spring but needs to be scarified before sowing. Seed is available from specialist wildflower nurseries.

▼ **Common restharrow (*Ononis repens*)**

Onobrychis viciifolia

Sainfoin

Description

RETAINING ITS French name (which means 'wholesome hay') from the time of the Normans, this stiffly erect perennial member of the pea family has long been grown as a fodder crop throughout many parts of Europe, including England. The pinnate leaves are about 10cm (4in) long and divided into many elliptical leaflets with hairs on the undersides. The robust stems are branching, the plant forming a small bush-like growth, topped with a profusion of round arrowhead–shaped racemes of dark pink flowers from May to August, each flower spike being about 5cm (2in) long.

How to grow

Height Up to 60cm (24in)
Habitat Found at field edges, roadsides and dry banks, often on limestone or chalk soils.
Garden care Water in well when planting in spring until it is established, but then only if the soil really dries out in the next few weeks. Deadhead regularly to prolong the flowering period and cut back hard at the end of the growing season.
Propagation Seed and plants are available from specialist nurseries. Seed can be saved from existing plants. Cuttings can be taken in summer and rooted in pots of sharp compost, sealed into plastic bags.

▶ **Sainfoin**
(*Onobrychis viciifolia*)

Knautia arvensis

Scabious (field)

Description

REACHING UP to 1m (3ft) tall, this is the largest of the native scabious species. Its lilac–blue flowers are up to 5cm (2in) across, though they lack the papery outer ring of petals of the garden varieties. Its hairy stems are surprisingly strong, and the stem leaves finely cut, though the basal ones are slender, undivided but toothed. All leaves are stalkless. With larger, paler flowers than the devil's bit scabious (p45), the field scabious is of similar maximum height and flowering season (from July until the first frosts) and also likes full sun. Naturally a meadow plant, it makes a very good specimen for the middle to rear of a border, where it can be combined with a range of other species to good effect. Small scabious (*Scabiosa columbaria*) is a similar species 30cm (12in) tall, with pale blue flowers.

How to grow

Height Up to 1m (3ft)
Habitat Meadows and grassland, including roadsides and dry slopes.
Garden care Can tolerate most soil types, although acid–free is preferable. Slugs can damage new growth in spring. Deadheading will keep the plants tidy, but makes little difference to the length of the flowering season.
Propagation Seed and plants are available from specialist nurseries. Seed can be saved from established plants. Clumps can be dug up and divided in spring.

◀ **Field scabious**
(*Knautia arvensis*)

Dipsacus fullonum
Teasel

Description

THIS STATELY biennial, much loved of flower arrangers, is also very useful in the woollen industry, for which it is still specifically grown in Somerset. This is for the rough, hooked bracts that are used to raise the nap on newly woven cloth. In its first year, it forms a rosette of prostrate prickly leaves up to 30cm (12in) long while its thick tap root runs long and deep into the earth. It is in the second year that the tall, branched stem rises up, angular, spiny and pale green in colour. The stem leaves are long and pointed, with spines on their undersides and often toothed edges, growing in opposite pairs from the stem. The oval flower heads are surrounded at their bases by small leaves and the pink flowers open in rings around the head, attracting bees and butterflies in profusion. Then the plant sets seed and dies, but the skeletal brown form remains over winter and often through the next year, providing a vital source of seeds to small finches through the cold months. Teasels flower in July and August and are ideal for the edge of a meadow garden or the middle of a mixed border, adding structure in a striking fashion from June onwards.

How to grow

Height Up to 1.8m (6ft)
Habitat Prefers waste ground, pastures and riverbanks. Tolerates wet or dry soil, but likes sun.
Garden care Take care to wear gloves when handling this plant, as it is spiny just about all over, but very little handling should be needed until it is time to tidy up the old, dead plants the year after flowering.
Propagation From seed, which is available from nurseries or can be saved from existing plants. Best sown where it is to flower, as the strong root system is not suited to growing in pots or trays. As for other biennials, sow in mid to late summer.

◀ ▲ **Teasel (*Dipsacus fullonum*)**

Vicia sativa
Vetch (common)

Description

THIS WEAK–STEMMED annual will sprawl over the ground or climb through other plants by means of the usual twining tendrils at the tips of the leaf stalks. The leaves are pinnate: the leaflets in three to eight pairs may be narrow and linear or oval, about 2cm (¾in) long. The pea–like pink flowers are borne singly or in pairs in the axils of the upper leaves and are up to 2cm (¾in) across. Widely grown as a fodder crop in the past, this plant makes an interesting addition to a raised bed or rockery, where the flowers can be appreciated close–up during the full length of the summer from mid May to September. There are several similar species that can also be used in the garden. The bush vetch (*V. sepium*) is of similar size with blueish flowers from May to July. The spring pea (*Lathyrus vernus*) is a 30cm (12in) high upright plant of deciduous woodland, often grown in the garden for its colourful purple and blue flowers in April and May. The meadow vetchling (p170) is of similar size and habit to the common vetch but has bright yellow flowers much like those of the trefoils from May to August. The yellow milk vetch has much paler yellow flowers in mid to late summer and grows in short grassland including on chalky soils.

How to grow

Height Up to 50cm (20in)
Habitat Likes grassland and footpath edges. Enjoys full sun.
Garden care Give the plant a sunny position and perhaps a spring–flowering plant for it to climb over. Deadhead regularly to extend the flowering period, like all members of the pea family.
Propagation Towards the end of the flowering season, allow a few pods to form and ripen. They are like small pea pods and go black when ripe. Collect the seed and sow when fresh. If you have to store the seed or buy it from a nursery, then a light scarification with fine sandpaper before sowing will aid germination. Seed is available from wild flower nurseries.

◀ **Common vetch
(*Vicia sativa*)**

Achillea millefolium
Yarrow

Description

THERE ARE numerous yarrows sold in garden centres and nurseries for the garden, with vivid colours through the range of yellows, oranges and reds as well as pinks and white. Most of these are not varieties of the native yarrow, but bred from two of the foreign species. However, there is a variety called 'Cerise Queen' which bears oval heads of deep–pink flowers and does originate from the native species. Our own yarrow usually has white flowers, though there are occasional pink and purple sports in the wild. The flowers form tight, branched heads very like those of the parsley and carrot families, but smaller and denser. These are held at the tops of the little–branched, furrowed and woolly stems with their small, feathery leaves from June to October. The plant is a perennial, the stems rising up from creeping ground stems each spring. The subtle white heads contrast well with more stridently coloured flowers in summer, such as purple loosestrife (p86) or some of the bellflowers.

How to grow

Height Up to 50cm (20in)
Habitat Can be found in meadows, woodland clearings, roadsides and dry grassland. Prefers full sun.
Garden care If you want the plant to grow in an exposed, open site, then it is best grown from seed where it is required. Otherwise it will need staking. However, in a more sheltered position or in a meadow environment with the support of other plants this will not be necessary. Yarrow can withstand dry conditions. It should be cut down to just above ground level once flowering has finished.

Propagation Seed and plants of the native yarrow are available from nurseries. Occasionally, the coloured varieties of this plant are seen in garden centres with the more usual cultivated ones of foreign origin. The plants can be dug up and divided every three years, basal cuttings can be taken in spring or seed can be saved and sown in spring, where it is to flower.

▼ **Yarrow (*Achillea millefolium*)**

Under the right conditions, wetland and marsh plants can look spectacular when allowed the room to thrive as nature intended, in great swathes of colour. Whether the space you can give them is large or small there are British wetland and marsh plants that you can enjoy and appreciate in your garden. Who could have a garden and not want to include the lovely yellow flag or the globe flower?

Marsh and bog plants

Growing wetland plants

BEFORE HUMANS started draining bogs and marshes for agriculture and for building land, such habitats covered large areas of Britain, but now only a fraction of that is left in isolated pockets, mainly though not exclusively in Scotland, Wales and northern and eastern England. Areas such as Tregaron Bog in West Wales, Wicken Fen in Cambridgeshire, the Somerset levels and the Norfolk Broads can be visited to see marsh and wetland plants in their natural habitat in safety. There are many other spots throughout Britain, some owned and managed by such organizations as local wildlife trusts, the National Trust and others. These are well worth visiting, especially during early to mid summer, when the butterflies abound and the flowers are at their best. This is also the environment of some of Britain's stranger natives,

such as the round–leaved sundew (*Drosera rotundifolia*) and its relatives, as well as some of the most beautiful, among them the wild orchids, and rarities like the pink–flowered marsh gladiolus (*Gladiolus palustris*).

Creating a bog garden

SOME MAY use the excuse that a bog garden is not easy to create in a garden where there is not a natural place for it, and it has to be said that it is easier to work with your conditions than against them. But a bog garden is no more difficult than a pond to create – easier, in fact, for you do not have to make sure that the liner will not get holes in. Indeed, it needs some holes for drainage, for the soil in it needs to be wet, not

▼ **Plan for a bog garden in early summer.**

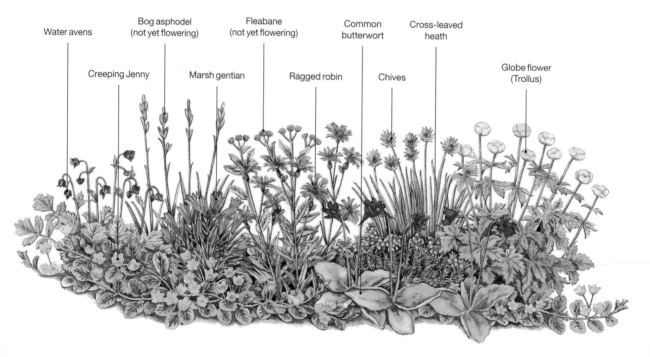

Water avens

Bog asphodel
(not yet flowering)

Creeping Jenny

Fleabane
(not yet flowering)

Marsh gentian

Common
butterwort

Ragged robin

Cross-leaved
heath

Chives

Globe flower
(Trollus)

stagnant. The bog garden can be linked
to a pond or it can be an independent feature.
It needs digging out to about 45cm (18in) deep,
then lining with a polythene liner or something
similar with several holes punched in it. It is
then filled in again with soil. If you want to
include some of the acid bog species, then mix
plenty of ericaceous compost into this. Soak
the soil well using the hosepipe before planting.
A mulch with bark chippings or cut reeds
will help to retain moisture by preventing
evaporation until the plants have established
and filled out. Then plants like shuttlecock ferns,
willowherbs (p90), fleabane (p84) and ragged
robin (p89) can be enjoyed in all their lush glory.

Growing in containers

For containerized marsh plants it is well
worth including water-retaining granules in
the soil so that it does not dry out, but no
other special consideration is needed apart
from plentiful watering.

▼ **Plan for a bog garden in mid summer.**

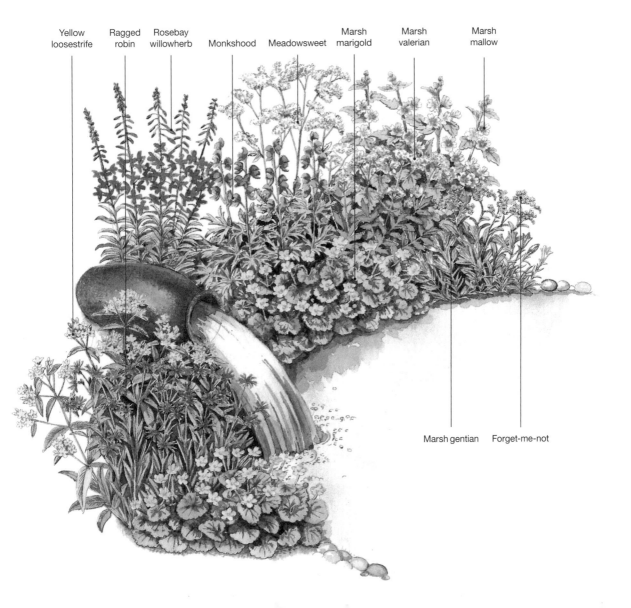

Yellow loosestrife · Ragged robin · Rosebay willowherb · Monkshood · Meadowsweet · Marsh marigold · Marsh valerian · Marsh mallow

Marsh gentian · Forget-me-not

Saving space

If you are short of space a plugged sink or a wooden frame lined with polythene or butyl can be used on a raised bed by the patio or even in an unheated greenhouse.

Plant choice

WETLAND PLANTS provide interest and colour for many months of the year, for the earliest begin to flower in March and several will continue into September or beyond. Then, through autumn and winter, interest is maintained by the evergreen rushes; the grasses which, though now only dead stems, remain upright; and the shrubs that enjoy this type of environment, such as cross–leaved heath (*Erica tetralix*), cranberry (*Vaccinium oxycoccos*) and bog myrtle or sweet gale (*Myrica gale*), among others.

There are so many beautiful wetland plants that it would be a shame not to include at least some of them in any garden. Some will grow in drier conditions as well as in wet soil, such as the yellow loosestrife (p87) and its low–growing cousin creeping Jenny (p83), as well as the willowherbs and meadow sweet (p88). These can be used to merge the wetland area into the rest of the garden. Others, though, are more strict in their requirements and with these, the soil conditions in which they grow naturally must be considered when choosing plants for your garden. Some plants are specifically adapted to the acid soils of peat bogs and sphagnum marshes, in the same way as the rhododendrons and camellias from Asia. Others can tolerate these conditions but are just as happy in neutral soils, and still others dislike acid soil

▼ **Plan for a bog garden in late summer.**

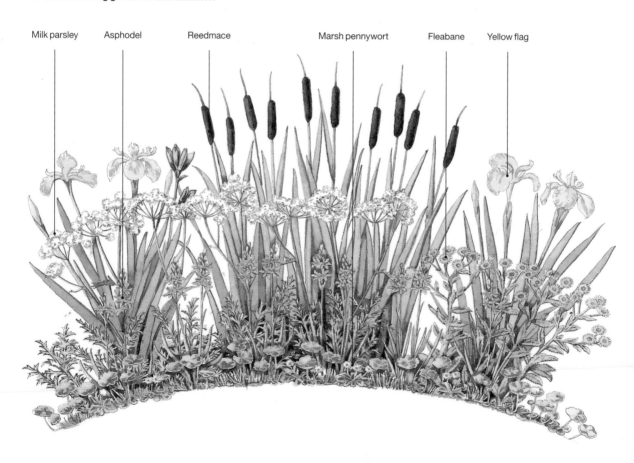

Milk parsley   Asphodel   Reedmace   Marsh pennywort   Fleabane   Yellow flag

entirely. Similarly, some plants like butterwort (*Pinguicula vulgaris*), marsh violet (*Viola palustris*), brooklime (*Veronica beccabunga*) and the common figwort (p84) thrive in damp shade while others need bright sunshine. Others like the marsh woundwort (p93) and the water forget–me–not (p102) can tolerate either.

Controlling growth

MANY MARSH and bog plants grow with vigour, so if space is tight there are two approaches to planting the bog garden. Clump formers and small plants like butterwort with its purplish blue flowers above yellowish leaves, the delicate–looking pink bird's–eye primrose (*Primula farinosa*) or some of the damp–loving gentians and wild orchids can be grown together in the same way as you would in any other garden border.

But the larger or more invasive growers like reed sweet–grass (p105), meadow sweet or hemp agrimony (*Eupatorium cannabinum*) can be used alone or in groups of two or three. Essentially, with these plants, you use the liner as a container in the same way as you would confine mint in a pot sunk into the ground. This should confine them quite adequately, but if you need some extra peace of mind in this respect then you can discourage them from spreading by surrounding the bed with a trench about 30–45cm (12–18in) wide and the same depth as the liner. This is filled with gravel which can be covered with a layer of compost or mulch to hide it, then any stray roots or rhyzomes that penetrate into it will not survive the adverse conditions it presents.

An alternative method of hiding the gravel trench is to grow low, spreading plants that will cover it. These can be planted in the edges of the bog garden itself. Useful plants for this purpose would include creeping Jenny (p83) or bog pimpernel (p89). Or the covering plants can be grown on the outer edge of the trench, in normal soil. Here they would include the dianthus species, common restharrow (p69), rockrose (p44), scurvy grass (p46), wild thyme (p50), wild strawberry (p49) and the stonecrops (p48), among

Upkeep of a bog garden

In summer the bog garden will need a good soak about once a week, but in the cooler months it will look after itself, provided that you keep the plants in order. Marsh plants tend to be vigorous, so keep an eye on this and keep things ruthlessly confined, trimmed and divided so that one plant does not out-grow and swamp the others. In this way our native wetland plants can be used to maintain a lush and potentially spectacular spot in the garden.

others. However, if the liner is placed in a mixed border among other plants of significant size, the trench is irrelevant as the plants outside the liner will be taking up enough moisture from the ground to discourage the wetland species from spreading beyond where they are required. In this way one can grow clumps of hemp agrimony, yellow flag (p113), woundwort (p93) or meadowsweet in the mixed border where they can stand tall among shrubs, meadow plants and even dry–ground lovers like sea holly (p28) and musk mallow (p24). In a similar way, the common figwort (p84) can be introduced to a shaded border, where it will make a subtle statement.

▼ **Drifts of meadowsweet, hemp agrimony, spearwort and marsh trefoil are punctuated with purple loosestrife.**

Geum rivale
Avens (water)

Description

R ED FLOWERS droop at the heads of erect stems, themselves a reddish colour, from May through to August. The basal leaves are large, rough and divided into broad lobes with serrated edges. They are soft and hairy and dull green in colour. Further up the stems, a few leaves are seen, much smaller and finer, divided into three segments and often a lighter green. This medium-sized perennial flowers copiously, the flowering stems much-branched and bent by the weight of the 2cm (¾in) wide, bell-shaped flower. They straighten again when the fruits form into burr-like, spiny, mid brown spheres. Closely related to the geums of garden border use, with their bright red or yellow double flowers, there are also two other native species. The wood avens (*G. urbanum*) is a common weed of gardens and waste ground with small yellow flowers at the tops of sparse, upright stems from May to August. The other species is mountain avens (*Dryas octopetala*), which is a small, attractive plant with eight-petalled white flowers from June to August, growing in highland areas of northern Britain.

How to grow

Height Up to 1m (3ft), but commonly half that.
Habitat Found by the sides of streams, marshes and damp woods, mostly in northern Britain. Water avens can tolerate sun or shade and any soil type, as long as it is water-retentive. Grows well in the herbaceous border on clay soils, but needs watering if the soil dries out.
Garden care Water in well when planting and if the soil dries out thereafter. Deadhead regularly to extend the flowering period and cut back the flowering stems in autumn.
Propagation Seed and plants are available from some garden centres and nurseries. Plants grow from an underground rhizome and can be divided in spring or autumn. Seed can be sown in spring to flower the same year, or in summer to flower next year. Sow in pots or trays or where the plants are required.

▼ **Water avens (*Geum rivale*)**

Lotus uliginosus
Bird's-foot trefoil (greater)

Description

LOOKING LIKE a large, often hairy version of the common bird's-foot trefoil described in the chapter on rockery plants, this perennial of the pea family has rather bluish-green leaves divided into three oval leaflets. The leaves are few for the size of the plant, which has long, hollow stems. The flowers, about 1cm (½in) long or a little more, are rich yellow and carried in round heads of eight or more from June through August. Each head is at the tip of a slender stalk up to 15cm (6in) long. Looks very decorative among rushes or reeds.

How to grow

Height Up to 75cm (30in)
Habitat Marshes, fens and damp meadows.
Garden care Deadhead regularly, cut back to ground level at the end of autumn and feed with organic fertilizer in spring.
Propagation Plants and seed are available from a few specialist nurseries. Seed can be saved from existing plants in the garden and sown in pots of damp compost in late summer or early autumn. Seed should be sown fresh or scarified before sowing – that is, the seed coat should be scratched to aid germination.

▶ **Greater bird's-foot trefoil (*Lotus uliginosus*)**

Narthecium ossifragum
Bog asphodel

Description

THE LIGHT green, sword-shaped leaves of this member of the lily family are arranged in two rows on the stems, becoming ever smaller as they near the flower spike. Once used in Lancashire as a hair dye, it is most common in the north and west of Britain, on upland bogs. It bears short spikes of star-like yellow flowers which mature to a light orange from early July well into August. Worth seeking out if you have a suitable home for it.

How to grow

Height Up to 30cm (12in)
Habitat Likes acid bogs and peaty marshes. Needs acid conditions and full sun.
Garden care Ensure conditions are suitable before planting. Deadhead unless the seed are required and cut the leaves down at the end of autumn.
Propagation Plants are available from specialist nurseries and some garden centres. Seed can be saved and sown in damp compost outside in late summer. Plants can be lifted and divided in spring or autumn, every three years or so.

▼ **Bog asphodel (*Narthecium ossifragum*)**

Petasites hybridus
Butterbur

Description

THE RHUBARB–LIKE leaves of this sturdy perennial can be seen commonly in damp places throughout England and Wales. The broad, palmate, mid–green leaves can be up to 1m (3ft) across, on thick, coarsely hairy stems which begin to grow at about the time when the flowers are open, in spring. Popular with bees, the flowers of both male and female plants are pinkish, without petals, each about 0.5cm (1/4in) across and borne in spikes up to 60cm (24in) tall. The female spike is a lot looser and less dense than the male, which is shorter and more rounded. Looks very similar to the huge, imported gunnera, but a fraction of the size.

How to grow

Height Up to about 1m (3ft)
Habitat Prefers stream and ditch margins, marshes and wet meadows in sun or shade.
Garden care This plant is fully hardy. The leaves can be cut off to the base at the end of the season for the sake of neatness and the flower stems can be cut back after flowering has finished.
Propagation Plants and seed are available from some specialist nurseries. Clumps can be divided, but the roots are substantial so it will take some digging.

▶ **Butterbur**
(*Petasites hybridus*)

Symphytum officinale
Comfrey

Description

RED FLOWERS hang in bunches from the axils of the upper leaves of this shade-tolerant plant. There is also a white–flowered and yellow/white–flowered variety. *S. asperum*, or rough comfrey, used to be widely grown as a fodder crop for cattle. Its flowers are blue but pink in bud, giving a two–tone effect. Another close relative is the naturalized Russian comfrey, of which there are numerous garden varieties available. Rough comfrey can take drier soils, but all need room to spread. The plants work well grown on stream banks or pond edges, where the ground is banked so that a lower viewpoint is available. Flowering season is from May to July.

How to grow

Height 1m (3ft)
Habitat Damp meadows, woodland, riverbanks and roadsides.
Garden care Comfreys tolerate shade well but do not need it. What they do like is a damp soil and room to spread. Their large leaves can make a good contrast to ferns.
Propagation Seed is available, as are plants, but the plants sold in most outlets are varieties of Russian comfrey mentioned above. For the native plant, you need to go to specialist nurseries. Plants older than two years can be dug up and divided in spring.

◀ **Comfrey**
(*Symphytum officinale*)

Eriophorum angustifolium
Cotton grass

Description

THIS RHIZOMATOUS perennial is classed amongst the sedges, which lack the swollen joints of the true grasses and have a triangular cross-section to the stems. It forms sparse tufts of growth with stiffly erect stems and narrow, grooved leaves which are sharply pointed at the tips. The flower spikes are short-stalked, in groups of three to five. They tend to hang down slightly and are a brownish colour when in flower, the characteristic cottony bristles growing out after fertilization has occurred. Cotton grass flowers in April and May; the short tufts of cotton, which wave and shake in the breeze, follow from May and last well into the summer.

How to grow

Height Up to 50cm (20in)
Habitat Found in bogs, pools and marshes, usually on acid or peaty soils. Enjoys full sun. Tolerates neutral sub-soil or planting compost.
Garden care Lift and divide every three years. Cut down dead stems as they appear, both for the sake of appearance and to prevent them from rotting in the water.
Propagation Available from some nurseries and water garden centres. Divisions can be replanted when plants are cut back every three years. Seed heads can be potted in damp compost and sealed in a plastic bag until germination.

▶ **Cotton grass**
(*Eriophorum angustifolium*)

Lysimachia nummularia
Creeping Jenny

Description

THIS HIGHLY adaptable plant could equally have been included in the chapters on rockery plants, pond plants or mixed borders. One of our prettier natives, it is usually found in damp places in the wild. The straggling stems have opposite pairs of rounded, bright green leaves and similar-sized, bright yellow cup-shaped flowers from May to July. The flowers grow on short stalks from the axils of the middle leaves, rather than towards the tips of the stems. Creeping Jenny can form a dense mat of foliage, spreading to about 60cm (24in) across. A golden-leafed variety, 'Aurea', is also widely available.

How to grow

Height About 5cm (2in)
Habitat Damp meadows, wet woodland and ditches in semi-shade, but will tolerate full sun. Can grow on the rockery, if the soil is rich.
Garden care Water in dry weather if placing in a rockery. Plants can be trimmed to size and the trimmings used as cuttings if required. Deadheading will extend the flowering season.
Propagation Available from garden centres and nurseries. Cuttings can be taken from non-flowering stems during the warmer months and rooted in pots of damp compost or a jar of water.

▼ **Creeping Jenny**
(*Lysimachia nummularia*)

Scrophularia nodosa
Figwort (common)

Description

THE MOST common of three figworts native to Britain, the common figwort has rectangular stems with short-stalked leaves in opposite pairs and a very loose, very branched flower spike. The flowers are small and greenish brown with a red upper lip that stands out well against the sky or open water. It flowers from June to September and, although not spectacular, is remarked upon wherever it is seen in gardens. It looks very good in combination with the yellow flag (p113) or yellow loosestrife (p87), for example. One of the other native figworts is the water figwort (*S. auriculata*), of which there is a very attractive variegated form available from nurseries and the larger garden centres.

How to grow

Height Up to 1m (3ft)
Habitat Wet woodlands, ditches and shaded stream banks.
Garden care Deadheading would be somewhat impractical with this one, but the flowering season lasts quite well anyway. A herbaceous perennial, it can be cut down to the base in late autumn.
Propagation
Plants and seed are available from specialist nurseries. Existing plants can be lifted and divided every three years or so, in spring or autumn.

▶ **Common figwort
(*Scrophularia nodosa*)**

Pulicaria dysenterica
Fleabane (common)

Description

THE BRANCHING, pale green stems of this perennial carry wrinkled, downy oblong-to-lanceolate leaves of the same colour, the bases of which clasp the stems slightly. The tips of the stems carry bright yellow, daisy-like flowers with large centres and short ray-florets from July into September. A very bright, decorative plant, it contrasts well with darker specimens, like the water mint (p88) or some of the rushes. Its name comes from the Middle Ages and before, when it was burned to drive fleas away from houses, though the effectiveness of this is not clear and it certainly attracts its share and more of insects when in flower.

How to grow

Height Up to about 60cm (24in)
Habitat Prefers wet woodland, ditch banks and marshes. Grows in light or heavy soils, in sun or shade.
Garden care Deadheading will extend the flowering season. The plant can be cut down to near the base at the end of autumn.
Propagation Available from specialist nurseries. Seed can be saved from existing plants in the garden and sown in pots in late summer, pressed into the surface of damp compost. Plants can be lifted and divided in spring or autumn.

◀ **Common fleabane
(*Pulicaria
dysenterica*)**

Trollius europaeus
Globe flower

Description

THE ROUND, globular flowers of this tall perennial appear – and in a few cultivated varieties, open – between April and July at the tops of dark, slender stems. The flowers are usually golden yellow, though there are pale varieties as well as orange ones in cultivation, for this is a popular garden flower as well as a native plant. Often, they appear not to open at all, staying round and globular, but in varieties such as the one illustrated, the petals do lay back to reveal the upright spray of anthers. The lower leaves are stalked and palmate, while those above are unstalked, three–lobed and toothed around the margins, arranged around the upright, often dark–reddish stems.

How to grow

Height Up to 75cm (30in)
Habitat Grows in wet meadows, damp woods and by streams, mainly in the north and west of Britain. Thrives in sun or shade.
Garden care Ensure when planting that the plant has a damp location and plenty of organic matter in the soil. Mulch in spring or autumn, water if there is any risk of the ground drying out in summer and cut back to ground level in autumn.
Propagation Plants and seed are available from garden centres and nurseries. Existing plants can be lifted and divided every three years in spring or autumn.

▶ **Globe flower
(*Trollius europaeus*)**

Cardamine pratensis
Lady's smock

Description

THIS PRETTY plant was once much more common than it is now. Also known as 'milkmaids' and 'cuckoo flower' in certain parts of England, it has pale pink, four–petalled flowers, borne in a loose bunch at the top of the slender stem from April into June. The basal leaves are pinnate or segmented; the segments small and rounded, in pairs, the tip leaflet larger, slightly toothed. The stem leaves are also pinnate, but the leaflets are narrow, almost linear, and the leaves do not have stalks. Lady's smock is a perennial plant, growing from a short rhizome.

How to grow

Height 20–40cm (8–16in)
Habitat Damp meadows, wet woodland, by streams and along shady lanes.
Garden care Ensure that the roots do not dry out, cut back the stems in autumn, and lift and divide plants every three or four years in spring or autumn.
Propagation Seed and plants are available from specialist nurseries. Seed can be saved from existing plants and sown in damp compost, the pots then sealed with cling film until germination has taken place. Plants can be divided every three or four years.

▼ **Lady's smock (*Cardamine pratensis*)**

Lythrum salicaria
Loosestrife (purple)

Description

THIS TALL, majestic plant grows in wetlands throughout southern Britain, as far north as south–west Scotland. Charles Darwin discovered that there are, in fact, three forms, which are different in the length of their stamens and styles and do not interbreed, but they have never been given different specific names. The leaves of purple loosestrife are dark green and hairy, the lower ones borne in whorls of three, gradually giving way up the length of the sometimes–branched stem to alternate pairs of leaves and then to the flower spike. This may be well over 30cm (12in) long, made up of whorls of flowers, each up to 2.5cm (1in) across and a rich, reddish purple in colour, though there are violet, pink and white forms. The hairy stems of this rhizomatous perennial become woody with age and are definitely square in section. The flowering season is from July to September. Various garden cultivars are available, including ones with pale pink and deep red flowers.

How to grow

Height Commonly up to 1m (3ft), but can grow to as much as 2m (6ft), especially if shaded.
Habitat Marshes, river and pond banks, ditches and wet meadows, though they can also flourish in drier conditions. A sunny position suits the plant best.
Garden care Water in well when planting; remove flower spikes as they die off, unless seed is wanted.
Propagation Plants and seed are available from nurseries and some garden centres. Seed can be saved in autumn and sown fresh in pots or trays outdoors for planting out in the following spring. Plants can be lifted and divided every three years.

▲ ◀ **Purple loosestrife (*Lythrum salicaria*)**

Lysimachia vulgaris
Loosestrife (yellow)

Description

IN COMMON with its close relatives, creeping Jenny (p83) and yellow pimpernel (p147), yellow loosestrife is a very adaptable plant. It is a herbaceous perennial which grows upright from creeping horizontal basal stems that root at regular intervals along their length. The upright flowering stems are unbranched and have downy pointed leaves, about 6cm (2.5in) long near the base, getting smaller further up the stems. The cup-shaped, bright golden–yellow flowers are in loose panicles, at or near the tops of the stems. They are open through June and July. There is a very attractive variegated form also available.

How to grow

Height Up to 1m (3ft), but often around half that
Habitat Occurs in wet woods, marshes, ditches and on riverbanks, but it will also grow well in drier places and can tolerate sun or shade.
Garden care Water in well when planting and in dry spells through the summer. Cut back flowering stems in autumn. Lift and divide every few years to keep the spreading habit in check.
Propagation Can be easily obtained from garden centres and nurseries, as plants or seeds. Seed should be sown in late spring or early summer in pots or trays outside, the young plants planted out in the following spring. Existing plants can be lifted and divided every two or three years.

▶ **Yellow loosestrife
(*Lysimachia vulgaris*)**

Caltha palustris
Marigold (marsh)

Description

ONE OF the earliest-flowering wetland plants. Its large, golden–yellow flowers brighten a sunny or shady spot from early April until late May or June and can sometimes continue until August. They are borne on branching stems that rise above the large, heart–shaped leaves. Plants vary greatly in size, leaves ranging from 7.5–20cm (3–8in) across. Early leaves, before flowering, are always smaller than those during or after flowering. The flowers look like large buttercups and the leaves are finely toothed around the edges. There is a white–flowered form, *C. palustris* '*Alba*', but this is less free-flowering than the original and a weaker plant. Also, a double form is available with the suffix 'Plena' or 'Flore Pleno' attached to its name.

How to grow

Height Up to 60cm (24in)
Habitat Found in wet meadows and woodland, by streams and ditches in full sun or partial shade.
Garden care Plant below the water line in the shallows of a pond or in the bog garden. Deadheading can extend the flowering season. Remove dead leaves before they rot.
Propagation Seed or plants are available at garden centres and nurseries. Plants can be divided in summer, after flowering.

▼ **Marsh marigold (*Caltha palustris*)**

Filipendula ulmaria
Meadowsweet

Description

YOU NEED to look closely at this substantial perennial to be able to tell which family it comes from, and then only when the flowers are fully open, for this sweet–smelling, foamy–headed plant is classified as a member of the rose family. The tall stems are dark reddish in colour and branched, the leaves dark green with greyish hairs underneath, divided into 5–11 segments, each roughly triangular and toothed at the margins. The tiny, five–petalled creamy flowers are carried in foamy heads towards the top of the plant from June to September, clumps of meadow sweet making a spectacular sight in damp meadows, ditches and alongside streams through the summer. There is a yellow–leaved variety available, 'Aurea'. Another, similar native species which grows on dry ground, often on limestone soils, is dropwort (*F. vulgaris*).

How to grow

Height Up to 2m (6ft), but often around 1m (3ft)
Habitat Grows in damp meadows, next to streams and in open wet woodland in sun or shade.
Garden care Add organic matter to the soil when planting, then mulch in spring. Ensure the soil does not dry out in summer and cut down the stems in autumn.
Propagation Plants are available from nurseries and garden centres. Existing plants in the garden can be lifted and divided in autumn or spring.

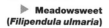

▶ **Meadowsweet**
(*Filipendula ulmaria*)

Mentha aquatica
Mint (water)

Description

THERE ARE well over a dozen species growing in the wild in Britain that are classified as belonging to the mint family, including herbs such as marjoram (p25), basil (*Clinopodium vulgare*) and the wild thymes (p50). Most of them, however, unlike water mint, like to grow in dry situations. This lightly hairy plant bears the characteristic smell of mint, especially when the short–stalked, oval leaves are rubbed between the fingers. It bears small, pink flowers in rounded terminal racemes from July into October.

How to grow

Height Up to 60cm (24in) if grown in shade or in close competition with other plants, but usually only about 20cm (8in).
Habitat Likes stream banks, wet meadows, marshes and wet woodland. Will grow in sun or shade, in wet soil or actually sitting in a few inches of water.
Garden care Like many of the mints, this one needs to be restricted if it is not to spread widely, so is best grown in a container of some sort, or at least a confined space. Can be affected by rust disease. If this is seen, infected leaves should immediately be removed and destroyed.
Propagation Plants available from garden centres and nurseries. Existing plants can be divided in spring or autumn.

◀ **Water mint**
(*Mentha aquatica*)

Anagallis tenella
Pimpernel (bog)

Description

CLOSELY RELATED to the scarlet pimpernel described in the rockery chapter (p43), this creeping perennial has tiny pink flowers in abundance from May to August. These are funnel–shaped, with five petals and pale, almost white, stamens. They are borne on 2.5cm (1in) stalks from the axils of the tiny, pale green, smooth and shiny round leaves, which grow in opposite pairs from the straggling, pale stems. The plants sprawl among other plants over the surface of wet marshes or pond edges, forming tight mats which can become up to 12cm (5in) thick if other plants allow them to clamber up as well as across.

How to grow

Height Up to 5cm (2in); but 12cm (5in) with support
Habitat Boggy ground, wet marshes and pond edges, usually in sun.
Garden care Trim to size if necessary in the growing season and cut back to the base of the stems in autumn.
Propagation Plants are available from specialist nurseries. Cuttings can be taken in spring or summer and rooted in damp compost, or seed can be saved from plants in the garden and sown fresh in summer.

▼ **Bog pimpernel (*Anagallis tenella*)**

Lychnis flos-cuculi
Ragged robin

Description

ALTHOUGH ITS Latin name means 'cuckoo flower' and relates to the time of year when it starts to flower, this is not the plant commonly called the cuckoo flower, the unrelated lady's smock (p85). The open pink flowers with their ragged–looking petals are borne in loose, branched bunches, mostly at the top of this red–stemmed perennial. The leaves are small, narrow and carried in opposite pairs, often tight to the branched stems and below the prominently displayed flowers. The flowers occur from May to August, though this can be extended another month by regular deadheading. They are very attractive to bees and butterflies. There is also a white–flowered form available.

How to grow

Height Up to 60cm (24in)
Habitat Marshes, damp meadows and wet woodland.
Garden care Deadhead regularly to prolong the flowering period and cut down the old stems in autumn.
Propagation Plants and seed are available from specialist nurseries. Seed can be saved from established plants and sown fresh in damp compost, outside. Plants should be lifted and divided every three years or so in spring or autumn, the divisions replanted and watered in well.

◄ **Ragged robin
(*Lychnis flos-cuculi*)**

Epilobium angustifolium
Rosebay willowherb

Description

NAMED FOR its leaves, which are reminiscent of those of the willow tree, this plant is one of several closely related species native to Britain. It has long terminal spikes of pink flowers, the four broad petals often divided from each other by the darker, purplish sepals, which are retained after the flower opens. The stamens are prominent and white, giving a hint of what is to come after the flower fades. The seed capsule and the seed bear long, downy hairs which give the plant an autumn appearance of having a thick, silvery coat of hair. Unlike the purple loosestrife (p86), the willowherb stem is not branched and the long, narrow leaves, carried in a spiral arrangement up the stem, are smooth. Also known as fireweed and French willow, this is a very adaptable plant and a quick colonizer, the wind carrying its seed into areas of felling in forests and into the rubble of destroyed buildings. Its close relative, the broad–leaved willowherb (*E. montanum*) is a common weed of gardens, having shorter, broader leaves and much less significant flowers. Great willowherb (*E. hirsutum*) is a sturdier–looking plant of similar height to rosebay willowherb, with larger but far fewer flowers distributed occasionally up the stem and in a loose group among the leaves at the top of the plant. Almost as common as rosebay willowherb and growing in similar situations, it is far less garden–worthy. There is a white–flowered variety of rosebay willowherb, which is very attractive.

How to grow

Height Up to 1.5m (5ft)

Habitat Clearings, footpaths, roadsides, waste ground and river and lake banks.

Garden care Deadhead thoroughly through the flowering season, which lasts from June to September, and cut down the stems to ground level in autumn. Lift and divide the plants every three years or so, digging in plenty of organic matter when replanting to encourage flowering.

Propagation Seed and plants are available from specialist nurseries. Seed can be saved and sown in pots or trays in late summer to be planted out the following spring. Plants can be lifted and the rhizomatous stock divided every three or four years.

◀ **Rosebay willowherb**
(*Epilobium angustifolium*)

Juncus effusus
Soft rush

Description

ONE OF the most common of nearly 30 species of rush that grow wild in Britain, the soft rush – like the vast majority of rushes – grows in wet places such as bogs and pond edges. There are two groups of rushes, which differ in where on the stem the flower cluster is held: the soft rush belongs to the group whose flowers are found part–way down the stem, rather than clustered at the top. It has a loose panicle, about 2.5cm (1in) across and yellowish green. Flowering is from early June to September. The pith–filled stems are the same dark green as the hollow, tubular leaves. It forms dense evergreen clumps, up to 30cm (12in) across, providing good colour contrast to paler–leaved or bright–flowered plants. There is a form of this plant whose stems spiral loosely known as the corkscrew rush, with the suffix 'Spiralis' on the name. This looks very effective against a pale background, especially when planted close to the corkscrew hazel (*Corylus avellana* 'Spiralis'), another rare form of a native plant recently popular in garden centres.

▼ Soft rush (*Juncus effusus*)   ▲ Corkscrew rush (*Juncus effusus* 'spiralis')

How to grow

Height Usually 30–60cm (12–24in)
Habitat Thrives in damp grassland, bogs and wet woodland. Can grow in sun or shade. A tough plant which will squeeze out competing plants from its space.
Garden care Lift and divide clumps every two or three years. Pull out dead stems to keep the plant looking its best. Remove flower spikes when over to prevent seed setting, unless it is required for propagation.
Propagation Plants sometimes found in garden centres and nurseries. Existing plants can be lifted and divided every two or three years; or seed can be saved and sown in pots outside in wet compost, sealed in a plastic bag until germination has taken place.

Ranunculus flammula
Spearwort (lesser)

Description

THE TWO native spearworts are very similar, except for their sizes. Both have slender, long leaves, pointed at both ends. Both have buttercup-like flowers from April to June. The greater spearwort (_R. lingua_) will grow in open water, while the lesser tends to be more of a marshland plant. The main difference, though, is in size. The lesser spearwort has flowers 2.5cm (1in) across and grows up to 60cm (24in) tall, whereas the greater is around twice as big. Both are very attractive plants, both to us and to hoverflies and other insects.

How to grow

Height Up to 60cm (24in)
Habitat Grows in marshes, fens and ditches, often in full sun. Can tolerate close planting.
Garden care Like most of the buttercup family, the spearworts have poisonous sap, so wearing gloves is advisable when handling them. Deadheading will extend the flowering season. The plants can be cut down at the end of the growing season.
Propagation Plants are available from nurseries and water garden centres, though the greater spearwort is more commonly available. Existing plants can be lifted and divided in spring, or seed can be saved and sown in pots of damp compost in summer. This is best done when the seed is fresh.

▶ **Lesser Spearwort
(_Ranunculus flammula_)**

Calamagrostis epigeios
Wood small-reed

Description

THIS TOUGH perennial grows from long rhizomes. The dark, greyish-green leaves are long, stiff and rough. They roll up almost in the manner of a rush in dry conditions, but flatten out again when the plant is watered. The flower panicle is large and dense, even when in flower during June, July and August. Also called bush grass, this darkly handsome plant grows naturally at the edges of woods, in ditches, scrubland and on wet ground, often in the shade. It forms large clumps if allowed to, but is well worth using as a background to brighter subjects, as well as in its own right.

How to grow

Height Usually 1m (3ft), but can be twice that.
Habitat Likes wet ground, often in shade, though it can tolerate a sunny site.
Garden care Lift and divide every two years to keep clumps to a useful size as well as making more plants, if required.
Propagation Seed is available from specialist nurseries or can be saved from existing plants and sown in damp compost sealed in a plastic bag until germination.

▼ **Wood small-reed (_Calamagrostis epigeios_)**

Stachys palustris
Woundwort (marsh)

Description

THERE ARE three species of woundwort in Britain, the other one that is commonly found being hedge woundwort (*S. sylvatica*). This has a longer, more slender and more sparse flower spike, usually of a rich, deep red, though there is a pink variety available. Also related are the grey, woolly, pink–flowered lamb's ears (*S. lantana*) and the native herb betony (*S. officinalis*). Marsh woundwort is a tall, slender plant which looks very like a large mint, with slender, lance–shaped leaves carried in pairs on very short stalks from the square main stem. The pink mint-like flowers, 1.5cm (½in) long, are carried in a dense spike at the top of the plant from mid June into September. All these plants are members of the mint family and share one important feature with the more commonly cultivated mints – the ability to spread by underground rhizomes. For this reason, it is important to be careful when placing them. They will not take over a border, but they will spread widely within in, pushing their way in like floriferous bullies among other plants. You can confine them physically within a container of some sort or you can simply be thorough in pulling up sections that have gone where they are not required. These sections can then be trimmed to size and used as cuttings if more of the plant is required for elsewhere in the garden or to give to friends and family.

How to grow

Height 60–100cm (2–3ft)

Habitat Wet meadows, marshes and riverbanks.

Garden care An organic feed in spring will encourage the plant to do well in summer, as well as lightening the soil, which it will welcome. Flower spikes can be cut back when they have finished to encourage more flowering and the whole plant cut down to the base later in autumn.

Propagation Plants and seed are available from nurseries and some water garden centres. Clumps can be lifted and divided in spring every three years or so.

▶ **Marsh woundwort
(Stachys palustris)**

Any garden is so much poorer without water that some form of pond or water feature is almost essential. Its calming influence is renowned: the sound of running water, be it a stream or a simple bubble fountain, is so relaxing. A water feature can be anything from a small pebble bowl or millstone with a pump and a little fountain to a large pond with fish and plants creating its own little habitat. There is nothing like good, clean water to bring out the best in your garden. All in all, a successful pond will repay the effort that went into its creation many times over.

Pond plants

Growing water-loving plants

F EW OF us are fortunate enough to have a stream at the bottom of the garden or to live next to the village pond, so any water feature in our gardens will have to be artificial. There are many ways of creating a water garden: it may be formal or natural, raised or sunken, with or without fish or frogs or other wildlife. The one thing that is essential is some form of sealed container. Any container, large or small, rigid or flexible, can be adapted to make a water feature.

▼ **Plan for pond planting in summer.**

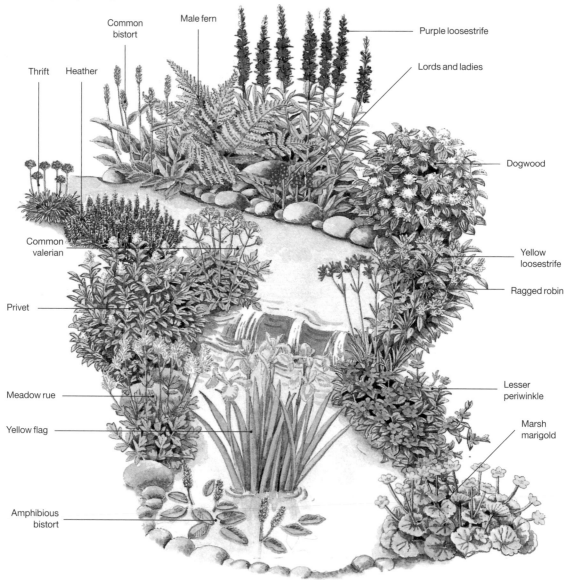

Common bistort

Male fern

Purple loosestrife

Thrift

Heather

Lords and ladies

Dogwood

Common valerian

Yellow loosestrife

Ragged robin

Privet

Meadow rue

Lesser periwinkle

Yellow flag

Marsh marigold

Amphibious bistort

Some plants can be kept quite happily in a half-barrel with a pump to move the water around so that it does not stagnate. Others need a large area to spread into in order to give of their best.

Creating a pond

Dig THE hole about 10cm (4in) larger than required, to allow for a 5cm (2in) lining of sand all over the inner surface. If you wish to keep fish, the finished pond should be at least 60cm (2ft) deep to protect them from frost during winter. Dampen the sand, then apply in handfuls and smooth over with the back of a spade, trowel or even your hands in those hard-to-access corners and angles. If you are using a flexible liner, cover the sand with some kind of

Siting a pond

Always dig a pond in a level area of ground. Whether you plan to use a solid or a flexible liner – or even no liner, if you live in an area of clay soil that can be puddled to seal it – you will not want it to show. Water is always level, so the edges of the recess you place it in must also be level!

outer lining. Materials are sold specifically for the purpose, but several layers of hessian sacking or some old carpet are just as good.

▼ **Plan for a medium/large pond in summer.**

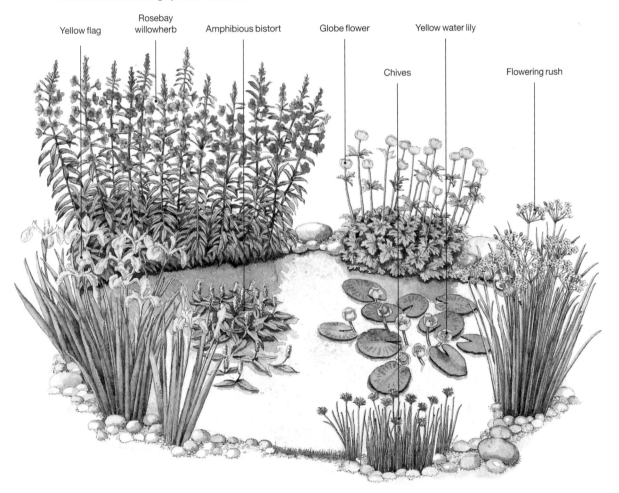

Yellow flag

Rosebay willowherb

Amphibious bistort

Globe flower

Chives

Yellow water lily

Flowering rush

Finally, add an inner liner of polythene or butyl. Butyl lasts longer, but is far more expensive. Polythene can be made more durable if all the edges are hidden thoroughly to protect them from the harmful effects of sunlight. This can be achieved with evergreen planting right to the edge, plus overlapping turf or stones. Allowing turf to grow right to the edge, or indeed to overlap the edge of the liner, works well, whether you want a formal or natural-looking pond, but the grass should be kept clipped at the edge. To provide a useful planting medium for marginal plants, and avoid the problem of losing soil into the water, turf can be turned grass–side down and used to overlap the pond liner then planted into.

Solid pond liners in plastic or fibreglass are not as easy to work with, but have the advantage of preformed designs with specifically designed planting shelves and pockets at various heights to accommodate a range of plants. If using one of these, then the outer liner of hessian or carpet is not needed, but you do need to be much more careful with the digging and the sand lining. All parts of the liner need to be supported – water is very heavy – so there will be a lot of lifting in and out, seeing where the liner touches the sand and filling in where it does not, then trying it again, all the time being careful not to

Pond compost

Do not use a rich planting mixture when planting anything in a pond. Pond plant compost is made up of mostly clay with very little nutrient value in order to maintain the freshness of the pond and not encourage algal growth. It is best confined in hessian with gravel on the top.

allow these adjustments to lift the liner out of level in any direction. After all this work, the edges will need to be covered in the same way as for the flexible liner, but the end result is more durable than either plastic or butyl.

More formal designs can include both sunken and raised ponds. These can be formed with brick walls topped with capstones. The liner – and these ponds are often shallower so better suited to butyl than plastic lining – is put in before the capstones are fitted and is backed with carpet or sacking as before. The pool is filled, then the edges of the liner trimmed to fit so that they can be folded under the capstones and cemented into place.

▼ **Plan for formal pond planting in summer.**

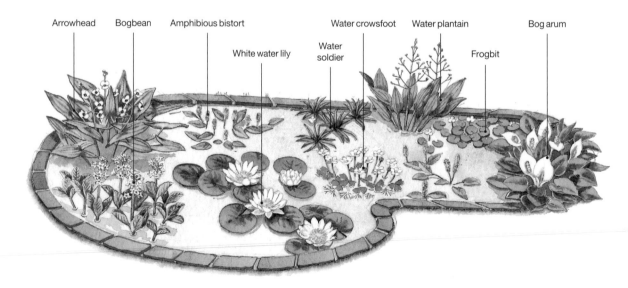

Arrowhead   Bogbean   Amphibious bistort   Water crowsfoot   Water plantain   Bog arum

White water lily   Water soldier   Frogbit

Keeping the water clear

ALL PONDS need either a pump or some oxygenating plants – preferably both in a garden-sized pond – in order to keep the water clear. Without them, algae will take over and you will end up with an opaque green and probably smelly mess, especially if it is populated with frogs, newts or fish, whose waste products encourage the growth of harmful algae in still water. Eventually, you will not only not be able to see the fish or frogs, but they will die or leave for more pleasant surroundings if the water is not oxygenated. But oxygenating plants are not restricted to Canadian pondweed and its relatives, which quickly become a nuisance by growing far too prolifically. There are also native plants such as the water violet (*Hottonia palustris*) and spiked water milfoil (*Myriophyllum spicatum*), which are much less vigorous and just as effective as well as being far more attractive to see, though they are not quite so easy to come by.

Plant choice

THERE ARE floating plants such as the water soldier and frogbit or shallow-water plants like the fringed water lily, water forget-me-not, water speedwell and, for larger ponds the amphibious bistort (*Polygonum amphibium*) as well as several others. Then there are deep-water plants such as the water lilies. Or, for a little bubble fountain, you can use plants that simply like a damp atmosphere, such as ferns and hostas. For a strictly native garden hostas can be replaced with lords and ladies (p145), pendulous sedge (p146) or comfrey (p82). All have their own place in the water garden, choosing them is simply a matter of scale and aesthetics.

Once the plants have established themselves, then wildlife will move in of its own accord and you may find frogs, toads and damsel flies populating your garden. Birds may drink from the feature or bathe in it, and night animals such as hedgehogs and foxes may do the same. Even dragonflies may visit, if only fleetingly.

Pests and diseases

Spraying anything in a pond should be avoided if at all possible. If plants develop a bad infection, remove the plant from the pond and install in a bucket for the duration of a more severe treatment. Any insect attack on pond plants is best washed off with a water spray: then fish and pond insects will eat the offenders.

Many water plants are vigorous growers, so will need to be lifted out and divided every year or two. This is best done in spring and clumps can simply be chopped into sections, the best of which can then be replanted into baskets with aquatic compost topped off with gravel and put gently back into the water.

Fish

DUE TO their shallow depth and wide expanse, raised ponds tend more heavily towards a growth of algae so it is more important than ever to either fit a pump and filter or get the balance of planting right before introducing any fish. However, if you are intending to stock the pond with fish, it should be remembered that a minimum depth of 60cm (2ft) will be needed to stop it from freezing solid in winter.

If you do plan to introduce fish into a new pond, you will need to wait for at least six months before doing so and then do it gently, floating them in a polythene bag in the pond for an hour to allow them to acclimatize to the temperature before releasing them. In an established, natural pond they will be able to look after themselves, but in a more formal setting they will need to be fed. Even in a natural pond this can make them more tame and willing to come to the surface where they can be seen and enjoyed, especially if you do it at a regular time of day.

Sagittaria sagittifolia
Arrowhead

Description

NAMED FOR the shape of its upright, long–stalked leaves, this is a close relative of the water plantain (p112). The first leaves to appear in spring from this sturdy perennial are grass–like, up to 1m (3ft) long and floating in the water. Then come the upright, triangular stems, each with its arrowhead leaf up to 30cm (12in) long. Lastly come the branching flower stems, up to 30cm (12in) above the surface of the water, with three–petalled white male flowers with black centres being carried above the spherical black buttons of the female flowers on the stems. These are carried from mid June well into August.

How to grow

Height Up to 1m (3ft) above the water surface
Habitat Ponds, canals and slow–flowing rivers in water up to 60cm (24in) deep but flowers better in water 15cm (6in) deep or less. Requires full sun.
Garden care Cut away leaves as they die back through the season. Cut down flowering stem when it has finished. If done quickly this will encourage further flowering later in the season. Cut back leaves to the base after they have died back in early winter.
Propagation Plants are available from nurseries and garden centres. Existing plants can be divided in spring or summer or new plantlets can be broken off in spring.

▶ **Arrowhead**
(*Sagittaria sagittifolia*)

Calla palustris
Arum (bog)

Description

THIS PLANT grows wild in a few lowland areas of Britain. It looks very much like a broader, shorter version of lords and ladies (p145). Its leaves are broad and rounded, the veins sweeping around towards their sharply pointed tips. The white spathe is shaped very much like the leaves and is quite open. The plant flowers from May to August, the flowers being replaced in autumn by the spikes of bright-red berries. The leaves can be evergreen in mild winters.

How to grow

Height Up to 30cm (12in) with similar spread, effected by rhizome growth.
Habitat Prefers pools, river shallows and boggy ground, either on peat bogs or in wet woodland. Can tolerate sun or shade, acid or neutral soil, but prefers shallow water.
Garden care Keep away from children as the plant, including the very pretty berries, is poisonous. Cut away dead leaves in winter before they rot. Trim to size if necessary in spring.
Propagation Plants available from nurseries and garden centres. Sections of rhizome can be cut away in spring and potted in wet compost to develop a good root system. The berries can be picked and sown in compost to germinate over winter, new plants emerging by late spring.

◀ **Bog arum**
(*Calla palustris*)

Utricularia vulgaris
Bladderwort

Description

ONE OF our native carnivorous plants, this is probably the least obvious of them. With finely divided leaves spreading through the water it has no roots, so floats at or near the surface. The leaves carry small bladders with hairy edges that trap and digest insects to help nourish the plant. The branching stems can be up to 1m (3ft) long, but are usually about half to a third of that. Reddish flower stems begin to rise vertically out of the water in June, each carrying several, bright yellow flowers into August. The plant is deciduous, dying back in winter and, like frogbit (p103), small buds fall to the bottom to overwinter, germinating into new plants in spring.

How to grow

Height Flower stems up to 30cm (12in) above the surface and spread up to 1m (3ft).
Habitat Ponds and lakes, in sun or shade, in water 15–100cm (6–36in) deep.
Garden care None needed once established, except for perhaps cutting off the flower stems when they have finished.
Propagation Plants are available from nurseries and some water garden centres. Cuttings can be taken in spring or summer.

▼ Bladderwort (*Utricularia vulgaris*)

Menyanthes trifoliata
Bogbean

Description

FOR MOST of the year this plant is recognizable only by the trifoliate leaves growing out from its thick, creeping stem. In May and June it bears spikes of pink or white flowers, opening from rosy red buds. The five petals of these are fringed prettily at the edges and surround violet anthers. Although the display does not last that long, it is well worth growing the plant for that alone – even without the attractive leaves. The leaves are borne on stalks up to 12cm (5in) long and each is divided into three smooth, oval leaflets. The creeping main stem can become very long.

How to grow

Height Up to 30cm (12in)
Habitat Ponds and the wettest parts of marshes.
Garden care The leaves are deciduous, so will need removing once they die back. The plant can be cut back in autumn or spring. These cuttings can be used, if taken while the plant is still growing, to make further plants by potting up in wet compost. Rarely, the plant may be affected by powdery mildew. If this is seen, affected tissue must be removed and destroyed immediately.
Propagation Plants are available from nurseries and garden centres, especially places specializing in water gardening. Cuttings can be taken in the warmer months, as described above.

▼ Bogbean (*Menyanthes trifoliata*)

Sparganium erectum
Bur-reed (branched)

Description

SWORD–SHAPED LEAVES up to 1.5cm (½in) wide rise from the thick rhizomes of this sturdy perennial. Robust stems grow between them, topped in summer by stiff, branching panicles of spherical balls of yellow–green flowers from June to August, followed by tightly packed bunches of tiny brown nutlets where the female flower heads – the lower ones in the panicle – were. This is not a showy plant, but sufficiently different to be interesting in the garden when planted in association with reedmace (p105) or yellow flag (p113).

How to grow

Height Up to 1.2m (4ft)
Habitat Shallow water at the edges of ponds, streams or lakes; also in wet marshland.
Garden care Can be susceptible to iris leaf spot, a fungal disease which is best dealt with by removing and destroying affected leaves as soon as it is noticed. Otherwise a very hardy plant, needing little care beyond making sure that it is placed in a suitable position in sun or semi–shade.
Propagation Plants are available from some nurseries and water garden centres. Existing plants can be lifted and divided in spring or summer. Seed can be saved and sown in pots of wet compost in late summer.

▶ **Branched bur-reed**
(*Sparganium erectum*)

Myosotis scorpioides
Forget-me-not (water)

Description

WITH ITS stem growing along the ground, sending out runners and rooting itself as it goes, this pretty little plant decorates the shady shallows of ponds, lakes, streams and rivers throughout the British Isles with its brilliant blue flowers from May right through into September. Although it roots from the stem as it runs, it never becomes a large plant or a nuisance, for if it reaches places where it is not required, it is a simple task to pull it up and cut it back. With larger, brighter flowers than the other nine species of forget–me–not growing in Britain, it is well worth including in any water garden feature.

How to grow

Height About 15cm (6in)
Habitat Shallow water, up to 15cm (6in), in shade.
Garden care This little perennial is surprisingly tough, but can occasionally fall victim to botrytis, or grey mould disease. If this happens, remove all affected tissue as soon as possible and burn or discard it. Deadheading will encourage a further flush of flowers.
Propagation Plants are available from nurseries and garden centres. In the garden, clumps can be divided in spring, or seed can be saved and sown in damp compost.

◀ **Water forget-me-not**
(*Myosotis scorpioides*)

Nymphoides peltata
Fringed water lily

Description

RELATED TO the bogbean (p101) rather than the water lilies, this floating plant looks like a miniature water lily until you look closely. Then you find that it does not rise from the bottom of the pond but instead has trailing stems at or near the surface, which root from the leaf axils. The leaves are rounded with the indented base of the water lily, but only 4cm (1½in) across, light green on the upper surface, reddish beneath. The bright yellow flowers rise up on stalks 5cm (2in) above the water surface, the five petals opening to about 5cm (2in) across through June, July and August.

How to grow

Height 5cm (2in); spread 60cm (24in)
Habitat Still water up to 45cm (18in) deep in sun or shade.
Garden care Can be affected by leaf spot, as can water lilies. Remove affected leaves immediately and discard. Trim stems back to size if necessary, though it never gets to be a very large plant.
Propagation Plants are available from nurseries and garden centres. Existing plants can be propagated by division in spring.

▼ Fringed water lily (*Nymphoides peltata*)

Hydrocharis morsus-ranae
Frogbit

Description

LOOKING AT first glance like a tiny water lily, the leaves of this plant are just 4cm (1½in) across, on stems only about twice as long as the leaves themselves. These grow from a central bud, along with trailing roots. The whole plant floats free in the water and is never more than 12cm (5in) across. Very rarely, it will flower, male and female flowers being on separate plants, with three white petals and a yellow centre. The flower is a little over 2.5cm (1in) across and held up 2.5cm (1in) or so above the surface. The flowering season is from June to August. In winter, the leaves are lost and the remaining bud sinks to survive the cold weather in the mud, along with other buds produced vegetatively from the roots. In spring, they grow leaves and roots and rise to the top again.

How to grow

Height About 6cm (2½in), all of which is at or below the water surface.
Habitat Sheltered standing water.
Garden care Allow this pretty little plant to float free on shallow water and it will help to provide shade for fish, but watch for snail damage.
Propagation Plants are available from some nurseries and water garden centres, though not reliably. As flowering is not common, reproduction is usually by vegetative budding from the roots in autumn.

◄ Frogbit (*Hydrocharis morsus-ranae*)

Eleocharis acicularis
Needle spike rush

Description

SOLD IN garden centres and nurseries as hair grass, this is a totally different plant from that delicate and pretty meadow plant. Tufts of fine, light green leaves, rolled like the other spike rushes, grow to about 30cm (12in) long from roots in the bottom of ponds up to 60cm (24in) deep. An evergreen plant, it produces oxygen from the leaves – as do all plants – which helps to keep the water fresh: it is sold for this purpose as an alternative to the ubiquitous Canadian pondweed. It is much prettier and less of a nuisance in the pond, though somewhat less effective on its own.

How to grow

Height 30cm (12in)
Habitat Ponds and lake shallows.
Garden care Little care is needed, beyond splitting the clumps every three years or so, before they break their planting baskets. Set the plants at a maximum depth of 60cm (24in), though it looks very good growing from a depth of about 20cm (8in), where it is deep enough to survive the winter freeze, yet shallow enough for the blades to lean and drift in the water.
Propagation Plants available from garden centres and nurseries. Can be lifted and divided every three years.

▲ **Needle spike rush**
(***Eleocharis acicularis***)

Carex riparia
Pond sedge (greater)

Description

THIS ROBUST tufted perennial with long, creeping rhizomes is a plant for the larger pond, unless you lift it every couple of years and chop it back to size. It is a handsome plant with stiff, upright, bluish–green leaves. The flowering spikes can cover anything up to a third of the length of the stem. There are three to six closely packed male spikes near the top of the stem and about the same number of thicker, dark green female spikes arranged down the stem. The upper one of these is stalkless and upright, while the lower ones have short stalks and droop away from the main stem. The flowers are present in May and June, with fruit following until September. The plant dies back in winter.

How to grow

Height Up to 1.5m (5ft)
Habitat Ponds and lakesides, streams and woodland marshes.
Garden care Plant between 10–30cm (4–12in) deep, near the edge of the pond. Lift and divide every two years to keep the plant down to size. Cut back dead stems in winter before they rot.
Propagation Plants are available from some nurseries. Divisions can be replanted in pond compost in baskets lined with hessian when the plant is cut back every few years.

◀ **Greater pond sedge**
(***Carex riparia***)

Typha latifolia
Reedmace (common)

Description

FOUND IN streams and at lakesides, this plant is often wrongly called the bulrush. In suitable circumstances it can reach 3m (9ft) high, but is more usually 1–2m (3–6ft) high. It forms a dense cluster of large, grass-like foliage, from the base of which rise flowering stems with the typical rich-brown cylindrical spikes of tiny flowers. The female flowers are towards the base of the cigar-shaped inflorescence, which can be up to 30cm (12in) long. A smaller variant of this species, dwarf reedmace 'Minima', is sold in garden centres and nurseries for garden use. Similar to its larger relative in every other way, it reaches just 1.2m (4ft) tall, so is good for a smaller pond.

How to grow

Height Up to 3m (9ft) but more often 1–2m (3–6ft)
Habitat Streams and lakesides on light soil, in water up to 1.2m (4ft) deep.
Garden care A plant for the larger pond, it will need dividing every two or three years to keep it in check, but nevertheless reedmace is a bold, stylish plant in the right situation. Likes a light, sandy growing medium. Best kept in a pond basket lined with hessian.
Propagation Plants can be bought from nurseries or garden centres. From then on, propagate by division.

▲ **Common reedmace**
(*Typha latifolia*)

Glyceria maxima
Reed sweet-grass

Description

THIS RHIZOMATOUS perennial is often seen growing in large stands on the rich mud of stream and lake sides, often in deeper water than other species. It grows 1–2.1m (3–7ft) tall, the long, broad leaves strongly keeled along the underside of the mid-rib. The flower panicle can be up to 45cm (18in) long and has many erect, spreading branches. It is pale whitish-green at first, ageing to purple through a pink stage so that the three colours intermix in a stand of plants in a very pretty manner. The flowering period is from June into August. It is a plant for the larger pond and, even there, will need cutting back every few years or it will spread extensively.

How to grow

Height Up to 2.1m (7ft)
Habitat Found at stream and lake margins, growing out into the water. Likes a sunny situation but is tolerant of most soils.
Garden care A soil deep enough to take a substantial root system is needed, as this is a tall plant and therefore needs to anchor itself well. Cut back clumps to a manageable size every two or three years.
Propagation Divisions can be replanted when cutting back or seed can be saved and sown in wet compost in late summer. Plants are sometimes available from specialist nurseries.

◄ **Reed sweet-grass**
(*Glyceria maxima*)

Rushes

THERE ARE around 30 species of rush that grow wild in the UK, ranging from a few centimetres to about 1m (3ft) tall. Most are perennial, but there are a few annuals among them. They are defined botanically by their flower structure, which has its parts grouped in sixes and, unlike the grasses, are recognizable as tiny flowers, though most are greenish, yellow or brown, so are subtle rather than bright and attractive. The rushes grow in damp or wet soil, in bogs or ponds. They are generally clump–formers, so can be introduced confidently into the garden. They are best lifted and divided every four or five years to maintain vigour and size as well as providing extra stock if required. Otherwise, as long as their roots are kept wet, the only maintenance they require is the removal of dead stems from among the clump. Being wind–pollinated, in most gardens they are unlikely to set seed, but if they do the seed pods can be removed once they are formed. You simply close your hand gently around a small clump of half a dozen or so stems and draw it upwards, pulling the seed pods away and disposing of them – unless the seed is required, when a few pods can be left to mature, then harvested into a paper bag.

Bog rush
(Schoenus nigricans)

SIMILAR IN appearance to the common spike–rush, the bog rush grows in dense tufts. The thin, stiff stems actually bear very small, bristle–shaped leaf blades, giving away the bog rush's relationship to the sedges rather than the true rushes. The flower head is carried at the tip of the stem and is narrow, spindle–shaped and rust–coloured, bearing slightly less prominent whitish anthers in May and June.

Common spike-rush
(Eleocharis palustris)

THIS EVERGREEN perennial is a clump–former like the other rushes, with leaves that are rolled into a tubular form up to 60cm (24in). It spreads by means of creeping rhizomes. The cylindrical spikelets of flowers form brown heads at the tips of the stems, decorated with many yellow anthers from May to July. The common spike–rush grows in marshes, ditches and pond margins. It is one of several spike–rushes found in Britain, but is the most decorative.

▼ **Bog rush (*Schoenus nigricans*)**

▼ **Common spike-rush (*Eleocharis palustris*)**

▼ **Compact rush (*Juncus conglomeratus*)**

Compact rush
(Juncus conglomeratus)

ALSO KNOWN as the conglomerate rush, this densely tufted perennial has finely striated stems, quite rough and matt green in colour with a continuous spongy pith in the centre, similar in many ways to the soft rush (*J. effusus*) mentioned elsewhere. Unlike the spike rush, the compact rush carries its inflorescence part–way down the stem, but in this case it is tight, rounded and dark brown, again flowering from May to July and naturally living in bogs, and also wet woodland and damp pasture.

Flowering rush
(Butomus umbellatus)

ONE OF our most attractive rushes, with tall, dark green, narrow leaves and 10cm (4in) heads of pink flowers that look like a very loose allium head throughout the summer. This is an excellent plant for the garden pond as, like many of the rushes, it forms a tight clump, rather than spreading as many of the reeds are inclined to do. In fact, this decorative perennial is more closely related to the lilies and orchids than to other rushes. The family also contains the arums, reedmace and common duckweed.

▼ **Flowering rush (*Butomus umbellatus*)**

Thread rush
(Juncus filiformis)

AS THE name suggests, the thread rush has very fine stems, growing up to 45cm (18in) long from creeping rhizomes. The pinkish–brown flowers are surrounded by a white perianth, giving the loose inflorescence a pale, whitish overall appearance. The flower head appears halfway down the stem in July and August. The thread rush is one of our less common rushes, though also one of our more attractive ones with its fine, delicate appearance and bright flowers. It grows well in damp, poor soil, often on stony lake shores and will thrive in a bog garden or in the shallows of a pond. Well worth its place in the garden, it will provide a subtle yet pretty foil to some of the more showy plants that can be used in these situations, combining well with the water forget–me–not, the bog pimpernel or the fringed water lily, for example.

▼ **Thread rush (*Juncus filiformis*)**

Ranunculus lingua
Spearwort (greater)

Description

VERY SIMILAR from a distance to the lesser spearwort (*R. flammula*) described in the chapter on wetland plants, the greater spearwort is larger and more often found in standing water, near the banks of ponds and streams. Like its cousin, it has lanceolate, pale green leaves held close to the stems and bears bright yellow buttercup–like flowers at the tops of the stems throughout the summer. These are up to 5cm (2in) across. This is a very showy plant when placed in front of something more subtly coloured, such as reedmaces (p105).

How to grow

Height Up to 1.2m (4ft)
Habitat Shallow water.
Garden care Buttercups are among the most resilient of our native plants. Placed in a suitable situation, little should go wrong with them. Deadhead the flowers to encourage production of more later and cut back hard at the end of the growing season, remembering to wear gloves as a precaution because the plants have poisonous sap.
Propagation Plants are available from nurseries and garden centres. Seed can be saved from existing plants and sown fresh on damp compost outside in late summer. Plants can be divided in spring or autumn, every three years.

▶ **Greater spearwort (*Ranunculus lingua*)**

Veronica anagallis-aquatica
Speedwell (water)

Description

ONE OF 18 species of speedwell native to Britain. Unlike most, but in common with marsh speedwell (*V. scutellata*), it has long, narrow, lanceolate leaves. The flower spikes grow up from the axils of the topmost pair of leaves. In the case of marsh speedwell, only one spike grows up from each stem, the flowers a pinkish colour. In water speedwell, however, two flower spikes are formed from each stem and the flowers are of the more typical blue, appearing from May through to October. Each flower is little more than the size of a forget–me–not flower, the spike being around 7.5cm (3in) long. Also closely related and available from water garden outlets is brooklime (*V. beccabunga*), which has dark blue, white–centred flowers in short spikes above shiny, green, oblong leaves.

How to grow

Height Up to about 15cm (6in) above the water surface when in flower.
Habitat Shallow parts of ponds and streams.
Garden care In common with several of its relatives, this is a semi–evergreen plant, dying back only in particularly harsh weather. Deadheading will encourage bushiness and more flower spikes later in the season.
Propagation Plants are available from nurseries and water garden centres. The wetland speedwells can be propagated from seed, summer cuttings or by division.

◀ **Water speedwell (*Veronica anagallis-aquatica*)**

Callitriche palustris
Starwort

Description

T HIS EXTREMELY variable little plant has been
called the chameleon of the water plants.
It will grow in up to 60cm (24in) of water or on
the pond margin, where it can form a mound
of mossy foliage up to 15cm (6in) high. Beneath
the surface, the stems are long and slender, with
narrow leaves paired at the joints, from where
fine floating roots also develop. Above the
surface the stems shorten and the leaves widen
into an almost circular shape, forming little
rosettes. The flowers are tiny, greenish–white
stars, appearing from May to September on
the sections above the water surface.

How to grow

Height Below the surface, up to 60cm (24in); on
the pond edge, 15cm (6in); spreads to 45cm (18in).
Habitat Still or flowing water, growing from the
pond or stream bottom or on the edge.
Garden care Clip surface growth back in autumn
to a few centimetres under the water: otherwise
the frost will do the same and make a sloppy
mess in the process. Trim to size when necessary.
Propagation Available from specialist nurseries
and water garden centres. Plants in the garden
can be lifted and divided every two or three
years or pieces about 7.5cm (3in) long, with some
water roots on, can be cut off and potted up in
wet compost
to make new
plants.

▶ **Starwort
(*Callitriche
palustris*)**

Nasturtium officinale
Water cress

Description

T HIS HAIRLESS perennial is the spicy, dark–
leaved salad plant. If picked from the wild
it should be washed thoroughly before being
eaten in case it is harbouring water–born
parasites. It bears small white flowers in a
flattened cluster from early June through to
September above leaves which are divided into
definite segments, each with its own central rib
coming off the main rib of the leaf. The clusters of
flowers are about 4cm (1½in) across, standing out
brightly in a shady spot in the shallows of a pond.
A related species, winter cress (*N. microphyllum*),
is also cultivated and crossed with water cress to
produce a late–harvesting variety for salads.

How to grow

Height 60cm (24in)
Habitat Shallow ponds and streams, also marshy
areas, especially on chalk or limestone.
Garden care Not suited to acidic or peaty areas, but
will thrive in sun or shade. Sun will produce better
leaves for eating, but in shade the flowers add
brightness. Deadheading will prolong flowering.
Propagation Plants are available from some
nurseries. Commercially, the plant is propagated
by cuttings
in summer,
but you
can harvest
and sow
the seed.
The plant
naturally
spreads by
creeping
rhizomes.

◀ **Water cress
(*Nasturtium
officinale*)**

Ranunculus aquatilis
Water crowfoot

Description

ONE OF several very similar species native to Britain, including the river water crowfoot (*R. fluitans*), this ferny–leaved perennial covers itself with white buttercup flowers from late April well into June. Closely related to the buttercups, the most important difference between those and the water crowfoots is that the latter are not poisonous: indeed, they are palatable and nutritious. The plants grow mostly submerged, usually in the shallower parts of ponds and lakes. The leaves are finely divided and can be up to 1m (3ft) long, making the plant quite substantial. In late spring floating leaves develop, along with flowering stems whose buds open into yellow–centred white flowers about 2cm (¾in) across. Definitely a plant for the larger pond, it is still well worth the space it takes up in early summer. The river water crowfoot is a larger plant, up to 5m (16ft) long and flowers later in the season, in June to August, but requires moving water to thrive and flower. Also similar is the white buttercup (*R. aconitifolius*) which grows up to 1m (3ft) tall in boggy meadows and by streams, in sun or shade. It has similar flowers to the crowfoots through the height of summer above pointed, tongue–shaped, mid–green leaves up to 6cm (2½in) long.

How to grow

Height Grows in water to about 60cm (24in) deep. Spread is up to 1.2m (4ft).
Habitat Still water, in sun or shade. Will grow in moving water, but will not flower.
Garden care Cut back to required size when it gets too large. Deadhead when flowering is finished.
Propagation Plants are available from some specialist nurseries. Seed can be saved from existing plants and sown in damp compost, covered so that it will not dry out. Clumps can be lifted and divided every two or three years.

▼ **Water crowfoot (*Ranunculus aquatilis*)**

Nymphaea alba
Water lily (white)

Description

THIS LOVELY flower is often grown in garden ponds, but has only two cultivated varieties other than the natural one – a pink–flowered one and a small–flowered one. The other water lilies grown in our gardens are generally of foreign origin, often oriental. The many petals of the white water lily open to a cup shape during the day, revealing the rich yellow boss of stamens at their centre until evening, when the flower closes and can sink below the water surface to re–emerge the following morning. Both flowers and round leaves float on the surface of still or slow–flowing water up to 3m (10ft) deep, the stalks growing up from large rhizomatous basal stems in the mud of the bottom. The scented flowers can be 20cm (8in) across and are displayed from May to August. The large leaves are deeply cut at the base, to where the stem joins. They are almost circular, reddish on the underside with a green upper surface and a leathery texture. They dot the surface of the pond through most of the spring, summer and autumn, dying back in winter.

How to grow

Height Can grow in water up to 3m (10ft) deep, the floating flowers being up to 10cm (4in) high.
Habitat Found in ponds, lakes and slow–moving streams or rivers.

Garden care Plant in a basket to restrict growth. Lift and trim to size every couple of years. Trimmings can be used as cuttings to start new plants. Can be attacked by a fungal disease called brown spot, which causes dark blotches on the leaves. Infected leaves should be cut away from the base immediately and burned. As a preventative measure old, yellowing leaves should be removed promptly and the water kept fresh and healthy. Water lily beetle can occasionally attack plants, leaving patches or wriggling trails of holes in the leaves. Adult beetles can also attack the flowers. The beetles hibernate over winter in poolside vegetation, so cutting this back in late autumn will help, as will regularly spraying the leaves with a water jet in the summer, as this dislodges the larvae, which will then be eaten by fish.

Propagation Plants can be bought from garden centres and nurseries. Existing plants can be lifted and divided every two or three years.

▶ **White water lily
(*Nymphaea alba*)**

Nuphar lutea
Water lily (yellow)

Description

LIKE THE white water lily (*Nymphaea alba*), this is a rhizomatous plant, growing in lakes, ponds or rivers. A similar species, also native, is the least water lily, which is like a small version of the yellow water lily, its flowers just 4cm (1½in) across and its leaves 10cm (4in) long. The leaves of the yellow water lily are up to 25cm (10in) long, oval in shape, rather than the round ones of the white water lily. The bright, buttercup–yellow goblet flowers, up to 7.5cm (3in) across, are displayed from June until the end of August.

How to grow

Height Above water, reaches about 10cm (4in), in flower: below water, up to 3m (10ft). Spreads up to 1m (3ft).
Habitat Naturally occurs in ponds, lakes and slow–moving rivers and canals, usually in sun though it can tolerate some shade.
Garden care It is susceptible to the same diseases as other water lilies, such as brown spot, lotus blight and attack by water lily beetles, all of which are best treated by immediate removal of all affected leaves and disposal by burning or in the dustbin. The main point of care with this plant is to keep it within the size limitations you have set, for it is a prolific spreader.
Propagation Available from some nurseries and water garden centres, it can also be propagated by division in spring.

Alisma plantago-aquatica
Water plantain

Description

LARGE, VERY open–branched panicles of tiny white three–petalled flowers decorate this rhizomatous perennial between June and September, the flowers opening only in the afternoons. The flowering stem can be anything up to 1m (3ft) tall and is leafless. The leaves, broad ovals pointed at both ends, grow on separate stalks from the base of the plant and have prominent parallel veins. Up to 20cm (8in) long themselves, they have stalks up to 30cm (12in) long. The flowers can sometimes be pale lilac or pink.

How to grow

Height Up to 1m (3ft) in flower
Habitat Shallow water at the edges of ponds, rivers, lakes and canals.
Garden care Plant in a water–garden planting basket so the plants can be lifted out easily for cutting back the leaves at the end of the growing season and for dividing plants every few years.
Propagation Plants are available from nurseries and garden centres. Existing plants in the garden can be lifted and divided every two or three years. Seed can be saved and sown in wet compost or soil in pots in late summer.

▼ **Water plantain (*Alisma plantago-aquatica*)**

▶ **Yellow water lily (*Nuphar lutea*)**

Stratiotes aloides
Water soldier

Description

THIS FREE–FLOATING plant, related to the frogbit (p103), though it seems entirely different until it flowers, looks like a pineapple head that has been dropped into the water. The stiff, sword–shaped leaves radiate upwards and outwards, up to 35cm (14in) long with sharp teeth along the margins. There are separate male and female plants. The flowers when seen – which is rare – are about 5cm (2in) across, white with a yellow centre and have three petals. Sitting low in the water, they grow from the centre of the plant from May to August.

How to grow

Height Up to 25cm (10in) above the water, similar below
Habitat Sheltered standing water.
Garden care This semi-evergreen needs little care once introduced, beyond occasional thinning out if it likes its situation sufficiently to spread. Generally grown for its structural impact rather than its flowers, which are not commonly seen.
Propagation Plants are available from nurseries and water garden centres. If they are happy, they will reproduce by budding from spreading stems. The buds can be separated in summer.

▼ **Water soldier (*Stratiotes aloides*)**

Iris pseudacorus
Yellow flag

Description

THE BRIGHT green, sword–shaped leaves of this handsome plant can be seen decorating the edges of ponds, rivers and canals from Scotland to North Africa. It is one of two irises native to Britain, the other is the stinking iris (*I. foetidissima*), which has short–lived purple flowers in summer, developing into bright red berries in autumn. The yellow flag is grown for its flowers, which open one at a time up the stem from May to late August. It can produce substantial stands, spreading with thick horizontal stems or rhizomes, regularly throwing up leaves and flowering stalks.

How to grow

Height Up to 1m (3ft), the flowers often standing up higher than the leaves.
Habitat Fens, reed–beds, riverbanks and pool sides, flood plains and wet meadows, in sun.
Garden care Irises will need lifting and splitting every couple of years to confine clumps to a manageable size. A rust disease can attack them. If caught early, simply removing affected leaves and destroying them will get rid of the disease.
Propagation Available at garden centres and nurseries. Plants can be lifted and divided every couple of years and repotted to form new plants.

▼ **Yellow flag (*Iris pseudacorus*)**

Whether you are growing a hedge, adding a few shrubs to a border to give it structure and winter interest, or doing the same for a rockery or scree bed, there is a wide choice among the forty-odd species that are native to Britain. Many have added benefits with the likes of crab apple jelly, elderflower or elderberry wine and cranberry juice all being produced from the fruit of our native shrubs.

Hedges and shrubs

Growing shrubs and hedges

SHRUBS CAN provide colour and interest at any time of the year, as well as helping to give the garden form and structure, especially in the colder months when the herbaceous plants are not there. Shrubs can also provide protection, as hedges, from prying eyes or invading footballs, and they are far better than fences in acting as a windbreak in exposed situations, for they filter the wind rather than blocking it and causing uncomfortable eddies. Of course, hedges take up more space in a garden than do fences, which can be an important consideration in a small space, but the variety and interest given in return is more than a fair trade–off against a couple of feet of border space.

▼ **Plan for a shrub area in late spring.**

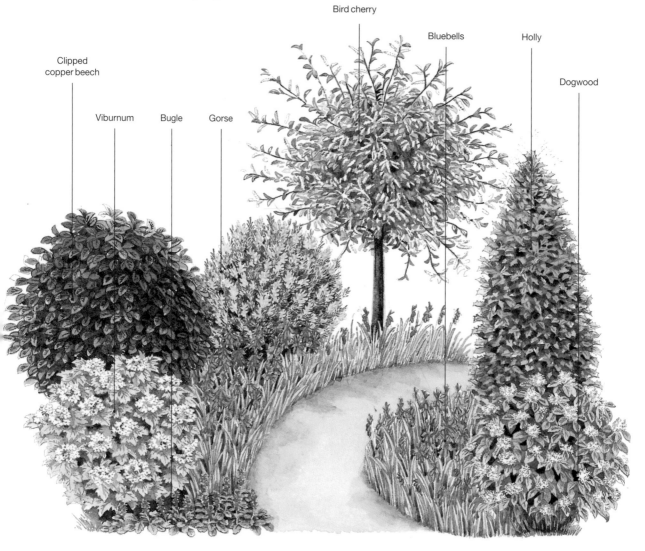

Bird cherry

Bluebells

Holly

Clipped copper beech

Dogwood

Viburnum

Bugle

Gorse

Planting a shrub

L IKE MANY trees, shrubs may be sold as potted specimens or as bare–rooted plants. Bare–rooted plants are generally found in nurseries through autumn and winter and should be planted immediately, unless the ground is frozen.

Whichever type of plant you are putting in, the most important element of the planting process is the hole. In order to allow the roots to establish well and provide firm support to the plant, they need plenty of room to spread. The hole should therefore be at least one and a half times as wide as you think it should. The base of the hole, once the correct depth has been achieved, should be chopped up thoroughly with the tip of a spade to allow root penetration downward. For potted specimens, the planting depth can be seen from the pot. Shrubs generally need to be planted at the same depth as they were grown. With bare–root specimens you should plant so that the junction between roots and main stem is at or just below the soil surface. With pot–grown shrubs, tease out any roots that

Delayed planting

If you can't plant your bare-rooted shrubs straight away, they can be stored in a bag of wet compost or in a bucket of water in the shed for a day or two. Indeed, soaking the roots in water for an hour before planting is good for them anyway.

are starting to go around the inner surface of the pot before planting. The roots of bare-root shrubs need to be spread out in the bottom of the hole.

You then fill in carefully between them, shaking the bush to feed soil between and among the roots as you go, then compacting it firmly at several stages during the process until you end up with the plant sitting in a slight depression in the ground so that water can accumulate around it and soak into the ground where it is needed rather than running off to beyond where the roots can reach it.

▼ **Plan for a shrub area in early summer.**

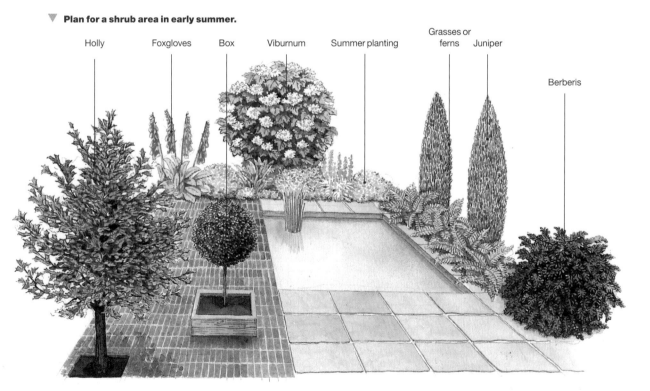

Holly   Foxgloves   Box   Viburnum   Summer planting   Grasses or ferns   Juniper   Berberis

Plant choice

To MANY people, shrubs are something that flower in spring, then sit there providing a green background to the flowering plants. How wrong can they be? You can have flowers on native shrubs from January to July by using the right combination, and that is without even using gorse (p123), which can be seen in flower somewhere in just about every month of the year.

By starting with blackthorn (p120) and butcher's broom (p121) and using mezereon (p128), hawthorn (p125), guelder rose (p124) and wayfaring tree (p132), then adding sweet briar (p131) and the burnet rose (p129), you can have shrubs flowering all through late winter, spring and summer and, by the time they are over, the first of the berries have coloured up on the guelder rose and perhaps a few early ones on the holly (p127) as well as the first hips on the wild roses. Then, as summer reaches its height in August and fades into September, the red berries of the wayfaring tree and the purple ones of the spindle tree (p130) come into their own. We have not even mentioned the evergreen bushes such as box (*Buxus sempervirens*), juniper (p127) and yew (p171), the silver leaves and orange berries of the sea buckthorn (*Hippophae rhamnoides*) or the autumn and winter colour of dogwood (p122).

▼ **Plan for a hedging and dwarf shrub area in early summer.**

Copper beech · Box · Broom · Mezereon · Cross-leaved heath · Juniper · Rockrose · Dogwood · Cranberry · Bearberry · Purple bell-heather · White rockrose · Heather

Many of the native shrubs are also useful in the garden, from the small, shade-loving butcher's broom to the viburnums – the snowball tree is a natural sport of one of the two British native viburnum species – and hawthorn, of which there are a number of extremely decorative garden varieties. These can be used in the shrub or mixed border or as a hedge and many respond well to clipping. Clipped regularly, hawthorn and gorse make surprisingly good, tight garden hedges that still give a display of spring flowers. The field maple (p164) also makes an excellent hedge and some of the classic hedging plants – yew, box, privet (p129) and holly – are natives.

Propagation

ONCE YOU have a shrub, it is easy to create more of the same. Hardwood cuttings, stripped from non-flowering stems about as thick as a pencil, preferably with a heel of bark from the larger stem that they grew out of are one method. They should be 10–15cm (4–6in) long overall, with two or three leaf buds as a minimum. The heel should be trimmed down to around 1cm (½in) long and can be dipped into hormone rooting powder if you wish, though this is not essential. All but the few leaves at the tip are stripped off then the cutting is pushed into a pot of damp compost, preferably mixed with grit, sand or vermiculite for drainage, or dropped into a jar with an inch or two of water in the bottom. Once rooting has taken place (easy to see in a jar of water, but you can tell in compost too – the tip will start to grow), then the cutting can be potted up individually and grown on until you are ready to plant it. Put five or six cuttings in a 10-cm (4-in) pot. Once filled, cover the pot with a plastic bag to retain moisture.

Another alternative for shrub propagation is layering. A branch is selected that is low to the ground. A sloping cut 2.5–5cm (1–2in) long is made lengthways part-way through the stem and passing through a bud. This cut section is then pegged down firmly into well-prepared ground. In time, roots will form at the cut and the new plant can be separated from the parent. If there are no low-growing stems, then a similar effect

▲ **Clipped box, juniper and willow combine with grasses for a monochrome study in form and texture.**

can be achieved higher up the plant by nicking a growing stem as before then bending it to keep the cut open without breaking it away from the main plant before wrapping the cut in a bundle of compost, sealed inside some polythene. This needs to be sealed tightly around the stem both above and below the wound as the moisture in the compost must not be allowed to dry out. Again, in time roots will appear in the compost within the polythene and the new plant can be cut away from the parent and potted up.

Shrub maintenance

NEWLY PLANTED shrubs, unless they are dormant as most bare-root plants will be at planting time, need regular deep watering, which is to say infrequent large quantities rather than a daily light sprinkle. Once a week or so except in the coldest weather, fill the watering depression, which only needs to be 2.5–5cm (1–2in) deep, let it soak in, then fill it again at least twice more. This should be continued until the plant is established and growing. From then on they should be able to look after themselves except perhaps in the harshest of dry or cold weather. You will just need to keep them pruned to the size and shape you require and dead-headed through the first half of their flowering season in order to prolong it as much as possible without impacting their fruit or berry crop later in the season. In this way, their value can be maximized in the garden and they can provide so much more than background and structure with an all-too-brief show of flowers.

Berberis vulgaris
Barberry

Description

THE BARBERRY was a common hedgerow shrub until it was discovered to harbour black rust, a disease of wheat. It was then torn up so is now rare in the wild. However, its highly decorative appearance has made it a prized garden plant. The native barberry has smooth, bluish bark and thorns arranged in threes on the stems, usually in the axils of the leaves. They turn a rich, orangey red in autumn, when the long, oval berries also ripen to scarlet. The flowers, in April or May, may be yellow or orange and clothe the bush in a blaze of colour for several weeks. There are a number of garden cultivars, including a copper-leaved one 'Atropurpurea', which is very attractive.

How to grow

Height Up to 3m (9ft), though it can be clipped to keep it smaller.
Habitat A plant of hedgerows and scrubland, preferring dry conditions.
Garden care Water in well when planting. Clip lightly when needed to save affecting the flowering of the shrub. If any rust is noticed, trim it out and dispose of the affected material.
Propagation Available from nurseries and garden centres. Can also be propagated from seed, planting the berries when ripe and allowing them to overwinter outside. Cuttings can be taken in summer or autumn and planted direct in the garden or in pots of coarse compost.

▶ **Barberry**
(*Berberis vulgaris*)

Prunus spinosa
Blackthorn

Description

THIS BUSH or occasionally small tree is also known as the sloe. Its dark blue–black fruits, which are too bitter to be edible when raw, are used for making wine and flavouring gin. The dark, thorny twigs form a dense tangle of growth which is almost impenetrable by anything but insects and the smallest birds. The blackthorn bears white blossoms with prominent red-tipped stamens on bare twigs from February to April.

How to grow

Height Up to 4.2m (14ft), though it can be pruned.
Habitat Likes woodland edges scrubland and hedgerows. Not very tolerant of waterlogged soil.
Garden care Firm in well when planting. Prune to size or a little smaller in autumn. Blackthorn is a relative of plums, apples and pears and so is prone to many of the diseases which affect them.
Propagation Plants are available from nurseries and some garden centres. There are several decorative sloe cultivars bred specifically for garden use, including the purple-leafed variety 'Purpurea', the double-flowered 'Plena' and the pink-flowered 'Rosea', as well as the wild type. All are best bought in winter and planted promptly. Cuttings can be taken and rooted in a spare corner to be lifted and moved as soon as growth shows rooting has occurred.

◀ **Blackthorn**
(*Prunus spinosa*)

Cytisus scoparius
Broom

Description

A GLORIOUS MASS of deep yellow flowers clothes this native of dry heath and sandy scrub in May and June. A branched and woody shrub, it has many upright green stems with relatively few and small leaves of a rich, dark green. These are three–lobed on the older stems, but simple, mid–veined ovals on younger growth. The flowers are pea–like and about 2cm (¾in) long, densely clothing the outer stems. There are many cultivated forms, some dwarfed for use in small gardens, others with different coloured flowers, ranging from white to deep orangey–red.

How to grow

Height Up to 2m (6ft), except cultivars of Warminster broom (*C. praecox*), which grow to 1m (3ft).
Habitat Found on moors, scrub and woodland edges, usually on poor soil and in full sun. Avoids lime or chalky soils.
Garden care Water in well when planting. Prune after flowering, but do not cut into older wood. Can be prone to blackfly in summer. These can be washed off or sprayed with modern insecticides that kill aphids without harming other insects.
Propagation Available from practically all garden centres and many nurseries. Half–ripe cuttings can be taken in summer and potted in a gritty compost, where they should root by late autumn.

▶ **Broom**
(*Cytisus scoparius*)

Ruscus aculeatus
Butcher's broom

Description

N AMED FOR its use in ancient times, this evergreen shrub is a rich, dark green in colour, the leaves glossy like those of holly (p127). An unusual point about this plant, though, is the fact that these leaves are not leaves at all but broadly flattened stems, the leaves being tiny, little more than scales in the junctions of these stems. This explains why the flowers are borne singly in the centre of the 'leaves', generally on the underside. They appear in February and March and though tiny – barely 0.75cm (¼in) across – are exquisitely formed. Lying flat to the mid–rib of the stem segment, each flower has six narrow white outer petals surrounding a purple corolla tube with creamy–white stamens at its centre. They are followed in autumn by prominent round red berries, about 1cm (½in) across.

How to grow

Height Up to 1m (3ft)
Habitat Shady woods and damp hedge bottoms.
Garden care Water in well when planting and ensure that it does not dry out too much in summer. In the unlikely event of attack by rust fungus, remove and destroy affected parts.
Propagation Available from some nurseries. Cuttings can be taken in late summer or autumn and potted in compost outside. They should be planted out before the winter cold sets in.

◀ **Butcher's broom**
(*Ruscus aculeatus*)

Rosa canina
Dog rose

Description

THE DOG rose can have pink or white flowers with a small, loose boss of yellow stamens in the centre and a faint perfume. Due to its loose habit and need for support from surrounding shrubs, the dog rose is often thought of as a climber, whereas the only true climbing British rose is the inappropriately named field rose (*R. arvensis*). The field rose has creamy–white flowers during July and August, while the dog rose flowers from late May to July. The hips of the field rose are much smaller than those of the dog rose. The advantage that the field rose has over other wild roses is that it will tolerate some shade.

How to grow

Height Up to 3.3m (10ft); field rose up to 2m (6ft)
Habitat Hedges and woods, preferring a sunny position, though the field rose will tolerate shade.
Garden care All roses can be susceptible to fungal diseases such as mildew and black spot, though the native ones less so than the garden varieties. Aphids and whitefly can also be a problem.
Propagation Some of the wild roses are available from specialist wildflower or rose nurseries. Hardwood cuttings can be taken and heeled in to root over winter with a bed of sand in the bottom of the hole. By spring they should be rooted and ready to transplant.

▶ **Dog rose**
(*Rosa canina*)

Cornus sanguinea
Dogwood

Description

THIS IS a native shrub that has made the move successfully into our gardens, where it is grown primarily for the autumn and winter colour of its stems, which vary from yellow through orange and brown to red, some with green leaves, others with a strong silver variegation. All look good throughout the year, with the narrowly oval, pointed leaves appearing in April, followed a few weeks later by flat panicles of white flowers in May and June. These develop into black berries, each on its own upright stalk, which contrast well with the rich red–brown of the autumn leaves.

How to grow

Height Up to 3.3m (10ft)
Habitat Woodland and shady hedgerows, though it can tolerate sun. Will grow in wet or dry soil, but prefers neutral or alkaline conditions.
Garden care Water in well when planting and firm the roots in. Clip the bush back every year for the first three or four years to encourage bushiness, then coppice every three years to keep the stems young and their colour bright.
Propagation Readily available from garden centres and nurseries. Semi–ripe cuttings can be taken in spring or summer while the plant is in growth, hardwood cuttings in autumn.

◀ **Dogwood**
(*Cornus
sanguinea*)

Sambucus nigra
Elder

Description

ONE OF our more common hedgerow shrubs, the elder is often used in the garden: it grows quickly, and bears good flowers and useful fruit. The leaves, larger and darker than those of the ash (*Fraxinus excelsior*), are divided into definite toothed leaflets. They have an unpleasant, rank smell, unlike the flowers, which smell sweet and fruity. There are several garden cultivars, such as the golden-leaved elder ('Aurea') and a number of dark-leaved forms, including the new 'Black Beauty': this has pink flowers, burgundy leaves and grows just 30cm (12in) a year, so is easily kept in control in the smaller garden.

How to grow

Height Usually around 2.1m (7ft) high as a shrub.
Habitat Grows in woods and hedgerows. Tolerates wet or dry soil, as long as it is rich in nitrogen. Can tolerate shade, but prefers sun.
Garden care Water in well when planting and if the leaves show signs of drooping thereafter. Elder can be coppiced every three years, if necessary. Contact with elder can cause itching in some people so wear gloves when handling.
Propagation Available from nurseries and some garden centres. Berries can be sown in pots in autumn to germinate in the following spring.

▼ Elder (*Sambucus nigra*)

Ulex europaeus
Gorse

Description

GORSE IS one of those plants that is essential for establishing a long season of interest, for although its main flush of flowers comes between February and the end of April, it is well known that you can find a sprig of flowering gorse somewhere at any time of year. Gorse's numerous spines and dense growth make it an excellent hedging plant. The long trusses of bright yellow flowers, interspersed with spines, are beautifully fragrant. There are two similar species. Dwarf gorse (*U. minor*) is a smaller plant, with shorter spines and deeper yellow flowers, and western gorse (*U. gallii*) is similar but tends to flower later, its main flush being in late summer and autumn.

How to grow

Height Up to 2.7m (8ft), except the varieties 'Flore Pleno' or dwarf gorse, which grow to about 1m (3ft).
Habitat Heaths, roadsides, banks and woodland clearings. Not on calcareous, or limy, soils.
Garden care Deadheading will extend flowering even more than usual. Clip to shape in early autumn. Can take fairly severe pruning, but this is best kept to a minimum if possible.
Propagation Both common and western gorse are available from nurseries throughout the country. 'Flore Pleno' is sometimes seen in the larger garden centres. Seed can be collected in autumn and sown either fresh or in the spring.

◄ Gorse
(*Ulex europaeus*)

Viburnum opulus
Guelder rose

Description

Its LARGE, palmate leaves with three or five pointed lobes can lead to confusion, especially in spring, between this and the wild service tree (*Sorbus torminalis*) or one of the maples. Unlike these, the guelder rose is a bush not a tree, and the leaves are broader than those of the wild service tree and more toothed than those of most maples. The main difference becomes apparent in May and June, when the guelder rose comes into flower. In its wild form, it bears flattened heads of white flowers, the inner ones tiny and numerous, the outer ring large, five-petalled and sterile. The whole head is around 7.5cm (3in) across, like a small hydrangea flower head, and they are borne prolifically over the surface of the bush. The name guelder rose correctly refers only to one form of the bush – the one most commonly used in gardens – which was discovered growing as a wild sport in Holland in the sixteenth century. This bears globular heads of flowers of the type normally around the edges of the rosette and is therefore sterile. It is commonly known as the snowball tree. The berries of the guelder rose, bright red in colour, are oval in shape and are beginning to ripen by mid-summer and contrast well with the dull loganberry red of the leaves in autumn. The berries show up even better after the leaves have been shed, but they are poisonous.

How to grow

Height Up to 4m (12ft), but more usually 2m (6ft).
Habitat Commonly found in hedgerows and still popular for the purpose, it is naturally found in damp areas including marshes and fens as well as in clearings in oak woods.
Garden care Pruning to maintain shape and size can be done in late summer, after flowering. Clearing up leaves after they have fallen is always a good idea, as it prevents the continuance of diseases into the following year and removes at least one hiding place for snails and slugs.
Propagation The snowball tree, being sterile, can only be propagated by taking cuttings, semi-ripe in late summer or hardwood in autumn, or by layering. This is a method in which a branch is selected and bent down to touch the ground, where it is pegged into place; usually the underside of the point of contact with the ground is cut part way through, if possible, just before a bud. This point will then root and the new plant can be cut away from the parent and moved to a new site. Similar methods can be used with the guelder rose, but in this case the berries can also be used. Like most berries, they need to be stratified (given a period of cold) to encourage germination.

◄ Guelder rose (***Viburnum opulus***)

Crataegus monogyna
Hawthorn

Description

ONE OF the earliest of the native shrubs to come into leaf in the spring: the early leaves are a fresh green colour, unlike those later in the season after flowering, which tend to be reddish. The leaves are roughly triangular in overall shape, but variously lobed, having anything from three to seven lobes. They are a little over 2.5cm (1in) long. The flowers come in May, in dense clusters along the branches, giving the plant its other name of May blossom. Hawthorn naturally forms a dense, thorny bush and can be used for agricultural hedging and, with careful clipping, for a garden hedge, forming a dense, neat growth. The autumn berries can be made into a sweet jelly. Left on the plant, however, they form a decorative red covering through autumn and well into winter, providing a food source for a variety of songbirds. Midland hawthorn (*C. laevigata*) is similar, except that it tends to form a small tree rather than a bush. It is more shade tolerant than the common variety and so is sometimes found in woods. It has a red-flowered variety 'Rosea pleno flore' and a variety of garden cultivars, some of which are crosses with the common hawthorn. There are white, pink and red-flowered varieties, some double-flowered, others single. All these different varieties of hawthorn make lovely ornamental trees.

How to grow

Height Up to 13m (45ft), if allowed, but commonly 1.5m (5ft) in hedge or garden use.
Habitat Commonly found in hedgerows and open grassland, also moorland and marshes.
Garden care Pruning is best done after flowering, as is the case with many shrubs, but that, of course, precludes the formation of the berries. If these are wanted, pruning can be left and done in the winter or in early spring, before the leaves come out. Flowering will be reduced as a result, but not entirely eliminated.

Propagation Pot-grown or bare-rooted plants are available from garden centres and nurseries. Cuttings are easily rooted. Hardwood cuttings should be taken with a heel, trimmed of excessive leaf and planted, preferably in a fairly free-draining soil, in summer or early autumn. Growing from seed is a more laborious method. The berries need to be picked in early autumn and stored in damp sand for eighteen months before they will sprout. They can then be planted up individually to grow into small bushes before being put out.

▼ **Hawthorn (*Crataegus monogyna*)**

Corylus avellana
Hazel

Description

T HIS USEFUL shrub bears its catkins throughout the winter, after the leaves have fallen. They appear in September or October and remain about 2cm (¾in) long until February, when they spring into growth, reaching about 5cm (2in). Near to them on the stem are the tiny red star–like female flowers. Flowering is over by mid–April and the leaves are then becoming prominent, growing alternately from the reddish–brown stems. They are broadly oval, with toothed edges and characteristic lop–sided bases. They turn a rich, warm yellow in autumn as the female flowers ripen into large round brown nuts, born on long stems in bunches of two or three.

How to grow

Height Up to 4.5m (15ft)
Habitat Hedgerows and oak and beech forests, where it forms a dense understory to the bigger trees. Tolerates sun or shade, damp or dry soils.
Garden care Firm in well and water thoroughly when planting. Prune to required size in summer, though you will lose that year's crop of nuts.
Propagation Plants available from nurseries and a few garden centres. Hardwood cuttings can be taken in late summer and heeled into the ground to root.

▶ **Hazel**
(*Corylus avellana*)

Calluna vulgaris
Heather

Description

O THERWISE KNOWN as ling, this largest of our seven native species of heather bears long spikes of pinkish–purple flowers from June or July right through September. It can be distinguished from its relatives by its tiny leaves, overlapping each other and set tight to the stems in groups of four. Also, its flowers tend to be on one side of the stem. Over time, the plant becomes woody and loses freshness, but hard clipping after flowering each year can prevent this. Heather flowers later than most shrubs and can give form to a garden.

How to grow

Height Up to 1m (3ft)
Habitat Heath, moorland and also pine woods. Needs neutral to acid soil and sun or light shade.
Garden care Make sure that you have suitable soil, on the acid side of neutral. If you have, they are not fussy about moisture content. Clip back hard, though not into old wood, in autumn after flowering is finished.
Propagation Heather can be bought as plants from a variety of outlets. Non–flowering shoots can be taken as semi–ripe cuttings in the warmer months and potted in sharp–drained compost to root in a few weeks. A 50:50 mixture of potting compost and sharp sand works well, watered thoroughly before inserting the cuttings and sealing inside a plastic bag.

◀ **Heather**
(*Calluna vulgaris*)

Ilex aquifolium
Holly

Description

HOLLY CAN grow into a fair-sized tree in the wild if allowed to, but is generally found as a shrub. This is almost invariably the way it is grown in our gardens. There are too many cultivated varieties to mention but the natural wild plant is as decorative as any. Its deep-green, waxy leaves clothe it thickly all through the year. They have roughly eight to 12 spine-like points arranged around their stiff edges and grow alternately from the dark-brown stems. Holly has small white flowers, held close to the stems, in May. On female bushes, these ripen to bright red berries by autumn.

How to grow

Height Can grow to as much as 18m (59ft), but can be clipped and shaped to whatever size is required.
Habitat Happy in full sun or in the shade of a forest, but dislikes wet ground.
Garden care Water in well and provide a low stake when planting the young shrub. Clip to size in August or September. Otherwise little care is needed by this tough and adaptable evergreen.
Propagation Available from garden centres, nurseries, market stalls and DIY centres. Berries can be planted, but will need a cold spell over winter before they germinate, which can take 18 months. Cuttings can be taken and rooted in the garden during the warmer months.

▶ **Holly (*Ilex aquifolium*)**

Juniper communis
Juniper (common)

Description

THIS SHRUB is one of two species – the other being the Chinese juniper (*J. chinensis*) – which are commonly grown in our gardens. One of Britain's three native conifers, the juniper can grow into a conical tree up to 6m (20ft) or as a low shrub with horizontally spreading branches. The leaves, or spines, of the juniper are short and sharply tipped, held out from the stem and often in threes. The berries, forming in late summer, are carried through the winter with a similar colour to the spines, but then ripen in the second year to a deep, bluish black. There are numerous garden cultivars, including the tall, thin 'Hibernica' and the low, spreading 'Depressa Aurea'.

How to grow

Height Up to 6m (20ft), depending on conditions and variety but more usually 30cm–3.3m (1–10ft).
Habitat In the wild, juniper is an upland plant, growing on moorland and downs. It can thrive in dry or moist conditions, in sun or semi-shade.
Garden care Water in well when planting, and it is worth keeping a watch on them for the first few weeks just to see that they establish well, but after that no care should be needed apart from lightly clipping if the plant gets too large.
Propagation Available from garden centres, nurseries and other plant sales outlets. Cuttings can be taken in summer and rooted in pots of coarse compost.

◀ **Common juniper (*Juniper communis*)**

Daphne mezereum
Mezereon

Description

RARE IN the wild, this upright, deciduous shrub is often grown in gardens for its sweetly scented, rich–pink flowers, which appear from February to April when there are still few, if any, leaves on the plant. Most of the long, tongue–like, dark green leaves appear after the flowers are over. They are up to 12cm (5in) long, with a strong central rib, wider towards the pointed tip. The small, red berries appear in late summer and autumn. They are poisonous to humans, though not to birds. The strong fragrance and bright pink colour of the flowers make the mezereon a welcome plant in the garden in early spring. There is also a white–flowered form called 'Alba'.

How to grow

Height Up to 1m (3ft)
Habitat Deciduous woodland, usually on chalk or limestone soil. The plant prefers at least partial shade and does not need a lot of water.
Garden care Once planted, the mezereon should be disturbed as little as possible. Pruning should not be necessary. It is not particularly long–lived and may need replacing after four or five years.
Propagation Plants are available from garden centres and nurseries. They are not easy to propagate. You could try a hardwood cutting in late summer, with sand in the base of the trench, but do not be too disappointed if it does not work.

▶ **Mezereon**
(*Daphne mezereum*)

Vinca sp.
Periwinkle

Description

TWO SPECIES of periwinkle grow wild in Britain, the greater periwinkle (*V. major*) which has flowers up to 5cm (2in) across and the lesser periwinkle (*V. minor*) which has flowers half the size. The former grows throughout lowland Britain, the latter just in the south of England. In both cases, the evergreen leaves are pointed, smooth and leathery, the stems lax and trailing. The blue flowers open in spring and occasionally through the summer from pointed buds in which the petals are twisted clockwise. There are variegated cultivars grown for garden use as well as the natural type with mid–green leaves. Either will root readily wherever the stem touches the ground, including in water.

How to grow

Height Up to 75cm (30in), though they spread up to twice that.
Habitat A very adaptable plant, naturally found in hedges and woodland edges, the periwinkle can grow in wet or dry soil, in sun or shade.
Garden care Water in well when planting and prune in summer to maintain the required size.
Propagation Available from garden centres and nurseries, the periwinkles are easily rooted by layering – pegging down a stem on to the ground, where it will root and can then be cut away from the parent plant.

▼ **Periwinkle (*Vinca sp.*)**

Ligustrum vulgare
Privet (wild)

Description

PRIMPRINT OR prim, as privet was called in earlier times, was used in gardens until the middle of the nineteenth century, when its close relative oval-leaved privet (*L. ovalifolium*) was introduced from Japan and found to be more reliably evergreen. The leaves are larger and longer than those of the introduced species, often curled upwards along the edges and are mid or dark green. It flowers in May and June, the tiny, sickly-smelling white flowers borne in small conical spikes up to 5cm (2in) long. The flowers are followed by a heavy crop of pea-sized berries which are purple when young, ripening to almost black and staying on the bush all winter.

How to grow

Height Up to 4.5m (15ft), though it can be clipped to any size below that.
Habitat Generally found in hedgerows, sometimes on waste ground. It tolerates dry conditions well.
Garden care Water in well when planting. If rust appears on the leaves, clip off and destroy the stems. Clip after flowering, preferably to a size a little smaller than you want.
Propagation Available from nurseries. Cuttings can be taken in the warmer months and rooted in the garden or in pots of compost. The berries can be picked and planted in pots outside, where they should germinate for the following spring.

▶ **Wild privet
(*Ligustrum vulgare*)**

Rosa pimpinellifolia
Rose (burnet)

Description

IT IS claimed that over 100 species of wild rose grow in the British Isles, but only five of these are commonly found and only four of those are available commercially. These can be split into pink ones and white ones. The commonest of the white ones is the burnet rose which forms a dense, spiny bush. It gets its name from its leaves, which are like those of the salad burnet. From May through to July it is covered in showy, cream-white blooms with the typical central boss of yellow stamens. These are followed by glossy, purplish-black hips in late summer and autumn. Its neat, dense habit makes the burnet rose a good choice as a hedging rose.

How to grow

Height Up to 1.2m (4ft) though often smaller.
Habitat Open, sunny situations, preferably on light, even sandy, soil. Tolerates wind and even salt spray, so is happy growing wild on sand dunes.
Garden care It will thrive in hot and dry conditions but can also be grown on clay. Dig in coarse grit underneath it and give it a generous planting hole. Like all roses, it can be susceptible to black spot and mildew as well as aphid attack.
Propagation Plants are available from nurseries. Hardwood cuttings can be taken in autumn, heeled in over winter in a trench with some sand in the bottom.

◀ **Burnet rose
(*Rosa
pimpinellifolia*)**

Euonymus europaea
Spindle tree

Description

DESPITE ITS name, the spindle is usually found as a medium to large shrub. Its smooth bark is greenish when young, maturing to grey; the branches are somewhat four–winged, as are the fruit and the flowers. The leaves are light green, thin and pointed, their edges finely serrated. In autumn they turn a rich, dark red, contrasting well with the pink four-lobed fruit. The bush flowers in May or June, the flowers having four narrow, white petals with four yellow–tipped stamens. The wood was used to make spindles for the hand–spinning of wool before the spinning wheel was invented.

How to grow

Height Up to 6m (20ft)
Habitat Hedgerows, woodland edges and scrubby slopes, particularly on chalk and limestone.
Garden care A low stake provided when planting will help to get the roots established, as will watering in well. Despite its delicate good looks, this shrub is relatively trouble–free.
Propagation Plants are available from nurseries and some garden centres. Bare–root specimens should be planted in winter, whereas pot–grown ones can be planted any time. Cuttings can be taken with a heel in late summer and potted to root over winter, or the seed can be harvested and sown in pots outside.

▶ **Spindle tree**
(*Euonymus europaea*)

Euphorbia amygdaloides
Spurge (wood)

Description

A MEMBER OF a truly worldwide genus of plants, the wood spurge is found in Britain with three other spurges, all small annual weeds of various situations. There are a few different varieties of wood spurge for garden use, including a purple-leaved one and a red-stemmed one. Actually a small shrub, the natural form has brownish–orange young stems and dark-green leaves that are long, slender and stalkless, growing in fives or sixes around the stems. The showy bracts are a pale, yellowish green, sometimes edged with red, and contain usually three tiny flowers. They give a good display through spring and early summer, and the evergreen nature of the leaves and stems adds form to the shade garden in the winter.

How to grow

Height Up to 75cm (30in)
Habitat Deciduous woodland, especially on chalk or limestone soils.
Garden care Water well when planting. Deadhead flowers if seed is not required, but wear gloves as the sap is a strong irritant. Keep away from the eyes and wash hands after handling.
Propagation Seed and plants are available from nurseries and garden centres. Seed can be saved from existing plants and sown fresh in the garden or in pots left outside over winter.

◀ **Wood spurge
(*Euphorbia amygdaloides*)**

Rosa rubiginosa
Sweet briar

Description

ALSO KNOWN as the apple-scented rose for the scent given off by the glands on the undersides of its leaves when they are crushed or wind-blown. This is one of the pink-flowered varieties of wild rose that are native to Britain. The flowers are similar in size to those of the dog rose (p122), but a darker pink with less prominent stamens. The leaves are paler and the hips more orangey in colour and round in shape. The sweet briar flowers in June and July and forms a denser bushy growth than the dog rose, so is better for hedging or in a mixed border.

How to grow

Height Up to 3m (10ft) if competition for light is strong, but more usually about 2m (6ft).
Habitat Grows in hedgerows and scrub. Tolerates most conditions, but prefers a heavier soil. Often found in southern England and the Midlands.
Garden care Most roses do not like dry soil. Any sign of aphid or fungal attack should be treated as soon as possible to retain strength in the young shoots and therefore flowering vigour.
Propagation Plants are available from some nurseries. Hips can be potted in the autumn and left over winter to germinate. Cuttings can be taken in spring or autumn and put into a trench with sand in the bottom. These should root in a couple of months.

▶ **Sweet briar**
(*Rosa rubiginosa*)

Hypericum androsaenum
Tutsan

Description

UNLIKE THE other native members of the *hypericum* family – the various St John's worts – this shade-loving plant is actually a shrub, in common with several of the introduced species which are widely used in our gardens. Tutsan has the characteristic bright yellow blooms with their prominent spray of stamens in the middle, though the flowers are no more than 2.5cm (1in) across. The leaves are large and oval, those towards the tips of the shoots having a reddish tinge to them. Overall, this small shrub has a soft kind of attractiveness that works well in most gardens.

How to grow

Height Up to 1m (3ft)
Habitat Commonly found in damp woods and hedge bottoms, it grows well in shade and can thrive in wet or dry soils.
Garden care Water in well when planting. Trim to size if necessary in autumn, after the fruit has set. Once established in your garden it will seed itself around freely.
Propagation Plants and seed are available from specialist nurseries. Soft cuttings can be taken in the warmer months and rooted in pots of damp compost, or the ripe fruits can be harvested and sown in pots to overwinter outside.

◀ **Tutsan**
(*Hypericum androsaenum*)

Viburnum lantana
Wayfaring tree

Description

THE COMMON name of this shrub is a corruption of the name given to it in the sixteenth century by the botanist John Gerard, who called it the wayfarer's tree because he found it to be so abundant along the old drove roads of southern England. Before that it was called the hoarwithy, for its downy white hairs on the undersides of its leaves and the willow–like suppleness of its stems. Unlike the other native *viburnum*, the guelder rose, this bush has thick, rounded leaves, evenly toothed along the margins and about 5cm (2in) long. They are borne in opposite pairs along the stem. The flowers are borne in broad, slightly domed panicles, 6cm (2½in) across and spread generously over the bush in April and May. The berries are slim and oval, starting off green and maturing through the late summer and autumn from red to shiny black. It is a dense, neat bush ideal for hedging, and can stand any amount of pruning or even layering, as has been done for centuries to field hedges. In these, the stems of the hedge plants are cut part–way through just a few centimetres up from the base and bent over, then tied into place to form a dense, even hedge.

How to grow

Height Up to 4.5m (15ft)
Habitat Found on field hedges, woodland edges and scrubland, usually on chalk or limestone, though it will happily grow on clay or loam. It is not found naturally further north than Yorkshire.
Garden care This resilient shrub needs little in the way of help from people, as it is ideally adapted for life in our climate. Pruning to size and shape can be done in late summer, when any diseased, dead or crossing branches can be removed for the sake of appearance. The plant can occasionally be attacked by black spot if it is stressed. This can be treated with a fungicide spray or the affected leaves simply removed and disposed of in the dustbin or by burning.
Propagation Plants are available from nurseries, though rarely in garden centres. Semi–ripe cuttings can be taken in late summer or hardwood cuttings in autumn. The seed, if used, needs to be stratified or given a period of cold before germination.

◀ **Wayfaring tree**
(***Viburnum lantana***)

Artemesia absinthum
Wormwood

Description

THE LATIN specific name gives away the primary use of this silver–leaved shrub as the flavouring for vermouth and absinthe. Having twisted, woody main stems, wormwood's main growth is much–branched and soft, with both stems and leaves silver in colour and silky to the touch. The leaves are much–divided and exceedingly soft. It bears yellow flowers in July and August, but is mainly grown for its foliage. Probably the best variety is 'Powys Castle', which has fine, lacy leaves and makes a good, robust plant. Wormwood is very attractive in bright sunshine and is also surprisingly tolerant of shade, despite its being a silver–leaved plant. Much smaller, but equally appealing and sometimes available for use in the rockery is the sea wormwood (*A. maritima*), which is just like a tiny version of the above, growing to just 30cm (12in) or so tall. Both these plants are essential for the sensory garden, where touch is so important. Wormwood makes a useful companion plant in the vegetable garden as its scent masks that of other nearby plants such as carrots and radish that root flies and other pests are attracted to. The leaves can be crushed and made into a useful plant spray against insect pests and the plant is sometimes used as ground cover to suppress weeds as its roots give off a chemical that discourages the growth of surrounding plants.

How to grow

Height Up to 1m (3ft)
Habitat Waste ground and dry slopes, usually in sun but tolerant of shade.
Garden care The one thing to note about the wormwoods is that they are easily starved and if this happens the lower foliage will die away, leaving a straggly brown plant with silvery tips. This can easily be avoided, by not leaving them in pots too long and by mulching with well–rotted manure or compost in the autumn.
Propagation Available from nurseries and some garden centres. Soft cuttings can be taken in the warmer months and rooted in pots of coarse compost. Seed can be saved and sown in pots outside in autumn or spring.

▶ **Wormwood
(Artemesia absinthum)**

Shade in the garden is not something to avoid or be worried about, but something to be enjoyed as a pleasant haven. As long as you choose your plants according to the situations they need to fill as well as according to your own tastes, there is nothing to worry about and plenty to enjoy. Every garden has a site for at least a few shade-tolerant plants. Even the smallest hedge, fence or wall, the side of a shed or the north side of an evergreen shrub can provide a growing position for them.

Shade-loving plants

Growing plants in the shade

SOME WOULD say that we seem to have more shade-loving plants in Britain than any other group. That may well be true, but it is hardly surprising when you consider that, before the interference of people, most of the British Isles was covered in forest of one sort or another. Many of those so-called shade-loving plants are no such thing. They are simply shade-tolerant and enjoy full sun as much as any of the meadow species, if they find an opportunity to grow in such conditions. Violets (p152), periwinkles (p128), the foxglove (p143), the bluebell (p140), the red campion (p59) and bugle (*Ajuga reptans*) as well as daffodils (p141) and ramsons or wild garlic (p149) will all grow as well in full sun as they do in shade. Others, such as the primrose (p148), lungwort (p146) and wood anemone (p140) grow better and more strongly in shade than sun.

▼ **A shady corner in May, brightened with a mix of woodruff, lady's mantle, lords and ladies and Solomon's seal.**

There is no need for deep shade in order to grow these plants. The sun can touch them for part of the day, as long as they have some shelter from it for much of the time. Growing such plants at the bases of walls, fences and shrubs is ideal, as well as under trees or at the base of a trellis. These are the plants that will brighten that dark, uninviting spot in the garden or grow lushly in a border where the sun-lovers become lanky and straggly for lack of light. They are the ones that make your sheltered, quiet spot in the shade into a green haven instead of a dark hole.

Success with shade

THE ONLY proviso to successfully growing plants in these conditions is that you plant them well. The planting hole should be backfilled with a generous helping of leaf–mold, garden compost or manure mixed in with the soil if it is at all dry and the new plants must be kept watered at least for the first six months if you are planting in spring. Watering is at least as important for these plants as for those in sunnier positions as, although the sun does not strike them directly, it is still at work through the surrounding trees and shrubbery, pulling water out of the soil around them. There is also the 'rain–shadow' effect to consider. Rain rarely falls straight down. Much more commonly it comes down at an angle so that one side of an obstruction like a wall or a tree trunk will remain dry, as will the ground at its base. However, diligent watering for the first season will see a plant through until it has a chance to get its roots down far enough to reach the naturally damp soil further below the surface.

Alternatively, you can sow seed directly into their growing positions instead of putting in mature plants. Sow in autumn and make sure the ground is damp before sowing. Scratch the seed in with a small rake or garden fork then cover with a thin layer of compost or leaf mould. The new plants will adapt much more quickly to their environment than potted plants would, delving deep with their roots for whatever moisture is available.

▼ **Shade plants for late spring.**

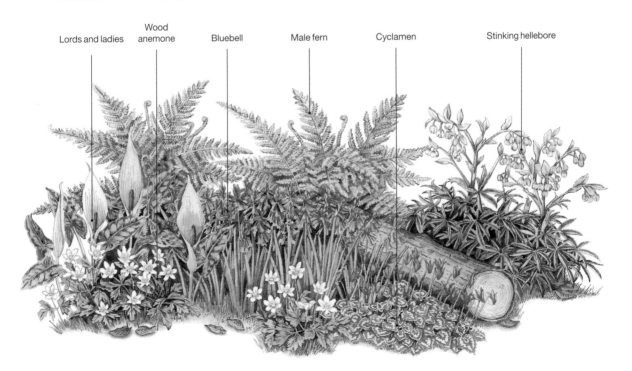

Lords and ladies   Wood anemone   Bluebell   Male fern   Cyclamen   Stinking hellebore

Keep soil damp

When sowing seeds, make sure that the ground does not dry out, watering if necessary with a watering can with a rose attached in order to avoid washing the seed out of position.

▼ **Shade plants for summer.**

Plant choice

A LTHOUGH MOST of the well-known shade plants are spring-flowering, there are plenty which go beyond that all-too-brief season, giving colour and form from January or February right through to September and beyond. In late winter the process begins with snowdrop (p149) and winter aconite (*Eranthis hyemalis*) and continues through the main spring flush into summer with plants such as lady's mantle (p23) and foxglove (p143), which can be seen in flower as late as mid to late August, the wood cranesbill (*Geranium*

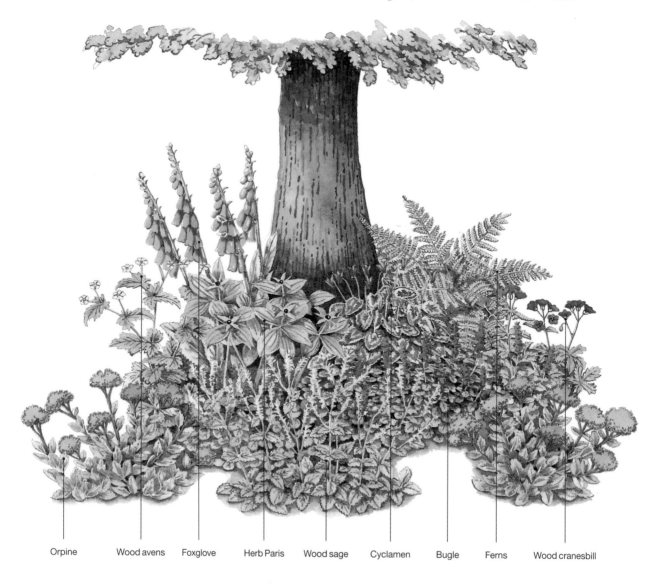

Orpine   Wood avens   Foxglove   Herb Paris   Wood sage   Cyclamen   Bugle   Ferns   Wood cranesbill

sylvaticum) and the yellow–flowered wood sage (*Teucrium scorodonia*), among others. We move into autumn with bugle (*Ajuga reptans*) and herb Robert (p144), both of which start flowering in spring and carry on pretty well right through, as well as orpine (*Sedum telephium*) and the native cyclamen (*Hederifolium purpurescens*), which flowers from June to September. Then, through late autumn and the depths of winter, interest can be maintained with the evergreen, sometimes variegated leaves of the periwinkles (p128), wood spurge (p130), some of the ferns and grasses and the strange, prickly shrub butcher's broom (p121) which flowers with the snowdrops, early in the year.

All these plants thrive in the kind of dry shade that abounds in British woodlands, yet there are plenty of choices for a damper shady site, too. Several wild orchids, the stinking iris (*Iris foetidissima*) – an unfortunate and largely unjustified name for this blue–flowered plant with its bright orange fruits that remain exposed through the winter – as well as many ferns including the unusual hart's tongue (*Phyllitis scolopendrium*), both the pendulous sedge (p146) and the wood sedge (p153), the dark reddish–leaved water mint (p88) and the may lily (*Maianthemum bifolium*), which looks like a cross between a wild orchid and lily of the valley, and many other plants will thrive in moist conditions.

Some, such as the yellow fumitory (*Corydalis lutea*), will grow in even the darkest and most un–promising positions, though this delicate-looking plant will also grow in full sun on a rockery or wall. There are also native British climbers and shrubs that will thrive in shade. Honeysuckle (p164) and ivy (p166) are both woodland plants and old man's beard (p168) will grow in sun or shade but, like other clematis species, prefers its roots to be in the shade. Box will grow in deep shade, as will tutsan (p131), wood spurge (p130), holly, mezereon (p128) and even the grey–leaved wormwood (p133) will also thrive in shady spots.

▼ **Catching only a couple of hours of morning sun, this spring border still sings with colour.**

Anemone nemerosa
Anemone (wood)

Description

A LSO KNOWN as the wind flower, the leaves of this common plant are divided into three coarsely toothed lobes, which are sometimes deeply split. There are three stem leaves, their stalks arising from near the top of the slender, upright stem, a short distance below the single large flower. The flowers have six narrow petals around a central boss of yellow anthers. They can be up to 4.5cm (1¾in) across and are open from March into May. Later, basal leaves arise singly on long, slim stalks from the narrow rhizome. There are several cultivated varieties of this plant, with flowers of pink or blue, including 'Robertsoniana' and 'Alleni', both of which are blue.

How to grow

Height Up to 20cm (8in)
Habitat Mainly found in deciduous woodland, but also in damp, shady meadows, often on alkaline soils.
Garden care Best planted 'in the green' – that is, in the growing stage rather than when dormant. Watering will be welcomed in a dry season, and a mulch with well–rotted organic matter will do the plants good as well.
Propagation Plants and seed are available from nurseries and some garden centres. Existing plants can be lifted and divided every three or four years, in early summer. Seed can be saved and sown in pots left outside over winter.

▶ **Wood anemone**
(*Anemone nemerosa*)

Hyacinthoides non-scripta
Bluebell

Description

T HE GARDEN variety of this bulbous plant is usually the closely related Spanish bluebell or a hybrid of the two. These are preferred because of their more even distribution of flowers around the stem, but are often less vigorous than the native, which can also sometimes be found in pink or white variant forms. These colour variants are rare in comparison to the usual rich blue, bell–shaped flowers hanging in umbels of anything from four to 16, on a stem that droops under their weight. Growing from the base of the plant are six to ten 28cm (11in) long, strap–like leaves, which last a good six weeks after the flowers fade towards the end of May.

How to grow

Height Up to 45cm (18in)
Habitat Deciduous woodland.
Garden care Shade–tolerant rather than shade-lovers, they like rich soil, but tolerate most sites and will self–seed if allowed. Rust can be a problem, but usually not until the leaves are beginning to die back anyway, so this is a sign that it is time to clear then burn the foliage. A light mulch with compost or chipped bark in autumn is welcomed.
Propagation Bulbs can be bought from garden centres or nurseries. Sow seed in autumn or keep it in a cold place for several weeks before sowing.

◀ **Bluebell**
(*Hyacinthoides non-scripta*)

Narcissus pseudonarcissus
Daffodil

Description

WHAT GARDEN could be complete without the bright presence of the daffodil to brighten the short days of February and March? The original wild variety, still seen in some areas of Wales and the West Country in woods and damp meadows, has scented, deep yellow flowers with a wavy edge to the 5cm (2in) central trumpet and blue–green stems and foliage. Now, however, there are an incredible number of varieties available. You can have daffodils in flower from January well into June, leaf colours from blue–green to yellowish and flower colours from white through cream to yellow and even pink.

How to grow

Height Up to 35cm (14in)
Habitat Grows in woods and meadows. Likes humus–rich soil and is both acid–tolerant and moisture tolerant.
Garden care Plant bulbs so that there is about 5–7.5cm (2–3in) of soil above their noses. Keep leaves on the plant for at least six weeks after flowering finishes in March or April. If space is needed before then, dig up and re–plant in an unused area of the garden until leaves begin to go brown.
Propagation Bulbs or plants can be bought in garden centres and nurseries in late summer or in flower in spring. Plant in autumn. Lift and divide clumps in late summer.

▶ **Daffodil (Narcissus pseudonarcissus)**

Circaea lutetiana
Enchanter's nightshade

Description

DESPITE ITS name, this delicate perennial is not a relative of the deadly nightshade (*Atropa belladonna*) or the woody nightshade (p167), but is related to the willowherbs. Its dark, slender stems carry pairs of long–stalked, pointed leaves around 10cm (4in) long. Above these, the stems branch to become flower spikes bearing loose, dainty spikes of white or sometimes pink flowers. The flowers are tiny with two deeply divided petals behind a pair of long–stalked anthers and an almost equally long stigma. Unlike many shade–loving plants, the delicate flowers come in late summer, when the shade of the forest is deepest.

How to grow

Height Up to 60cm (24in), often closer to 40cm (16in)
Habitat Shady hedge bottoms and woodland floors, in damp or dry conditions.
Garden care This plant grows up each year from a rhizome that is not easy to eradicate. Cut down to the base in late autumn. Deadhead to extend flowering season and prevent seeding.
Propagation Available as plants or seed from some specialist nurseries. The seed heads can be saved and sown in late summer or early autumn, then left to germinate in the spring. Clumps can be lifted and divided every few years.

◀ **Enchanter's nightshade (Circaea lutetiana)**

Dryopteris felix-mas
Fern (male)

Description

THE MALE fern's name has nothing to do with its gender, but was a way of identifying it from the similar lady fern, which is more finely divided, delicate and 'feminine'. Both have the typical fern structure: several leaves arising from a central point, each one divided into leaflets along its main stalk, each of those leaflets divided again along its own central rib. The whole leaf is shaped so that it widens from the base to about two-thirds of the way along, then tapers sharply back to a pointed tip. The male fern is one of our larger ferns, its tall shuttlecocks of leaves, darker on the upper surface than underneath and quite upright when young. Later in the year, the spores form dark-brown lines along the undersides of the ribs of the leaflets.

How to grow

Height Up to 1.5m (5ft)
Habitat Woodland, shady ditches and hedgerows and sometimes among boulders by streams.
Garden care Choose a site with some shade and dampness. Soil does not have to be deep, but needs to be moisture-retentive. Remove old leaves after new ones have grown in late spring.
Propagation Ferns propagate by means of spores on the undersides of the leaves. When these become ripe, a few leaflets can be picked and pegged down, right-side-up, on to moist compost. If the pots are left in a cool, damp place, then germination should take place.

▶ **Male fern (*Dryopteris felix-mas*)**

Myosotis sylvatica
Forget-me-not (wood)

Description

BY FAR the prettier of our two dry-land species of forget-me-not, the other being the common variety (*M. arvensis*). The wood forget-me-not is a bushy mid-green plant, hairy, with elliptical leaves which are stalkless and carried alternately on the branching stems. At and near the top of the plant are loose bunches of sky-blue flowers, with bright yellow centres. Flowering is from April or May to July. This lovely little plant combines wonderfully with a range of different flowers in the garden, such as the tulips, wallflowers or primulas and a smaller introduced species (*M. alpestris*).

How to grow

Height Up to 35cm (14in)
Habitat Occurs in open woodland, on damp or dry soils. Can tolerate neutral or alkaline soils. Prefers at least some shade.
Garden care These easy-to-grow plants require little care, except for watering in hot weather and a little deadheading. Replace the plants each year.
Propagation Best grown as a biennial, plants and seed are readily available in nurseries and garden centres. Seed can be saved from plants in the garden. It should be sown in pots or trays in summer, ready for planting out in autumn or early spring.

◀ **Wood forget-me-not (*Myosotis sylvatica*)**

Digitalis purpurea
Foxglove

Description

O NE OF the cottage garden classics, this tall, stately plant is tolerant of a wide range of conditions, from damp woods to sun–drenched stone walls. There are dozens of different species and garden varieties of foxglove, from white, through yellow and cream to pinks and purples, and 30cm–1.5m (12in–5ft) in height. In recent times, the garden varieties have become much more densely flowered and showy, but the basic native purple foxglove still has a charm all of its own. The tubular flowers, often with spotted markings inside the lower lip, are borne in one to three columns, generally up one side of the tall flowering stem from late May through to August. The greyish–green, felty leaves form a rosette close to the ground in the first year, then send up a single stem during the second year, the lower portion of which has leaves smaller than those of the rosette below a long spike of flowers. The plant will seed copiously, but if allowed to do so it will then die, as all biennials do. If, however, the flower spike is removed as soon as the flowers fade, it will live on to flower another year. In this way, plants can be kept for up to three or four years.

How to grow

Height Up to 1.5m (5ft), though some varieties are shorter.
Habitat Generally thought of as a plant of woodlands, but also found growing wild on rocky scree and even on stone walls. Happy in sun or shade, but the garden hybrids especially do like some dampness.
Garden care If you are growing garden hybrids, water in dry weather. If growing the native plant, then water if it begins to droop. Otherwise, foxgloves are tough and hardy plants: most soils and situations will do, though they grow especially well if given a reasonably rich soil and some shade.
Propagation Seed and plants are widely available from nurseries, garden centres and market stalls, especially in spring. Seed, whether bought or saved from your own plants, should be sown in spring or early summer and planted out where they are to flower in autumn, when they are 5cm (2in) high or more.

▶ **Foxglove (*Digitalis purpurea*)**

Geranium robertianum
Herb Robert

Description

ONE OF our prettier wild flowers, this annual geranium has dark–green or more usually red stems and bright green leaves, finely divided to give an almost ferny effect, topped by bright pink buds. It flowers from May right through to December, if the weather is sufficiently mild. The whole plant is covered with fine, short, silvery hairs which are displayed admirably when the light is behind them. It is a very widespread plant, being distributed almost all over the northern hemisphere, probably because it is so adaptable in its choice of home. It is equally at home in sun or shade, in moist or dry conditions, its fairly lax stems growing through and around other plants to achieve their maximum height. If no support is available it will stay small and compact in sun or shade. It looks lovely on the rockery in combination with thrift or on the shaded back of a stone wall, along with maidenhair spleenwort. Alternatively, it can brighten up a shady woodland site after the bluebells have finished their display, either on its own or combined with bugle or stitchwort.

How to grow

Height Up to 50cm (20in)

Habitat Likes woods, grassland, walls and seashore, usually, but not always, on neutral to limy soil. Herb Robert grows well in either sunny or shady conditions.

Garden care Very little can go wrong with this most adaptable plant, once it is established. Sow seeds in autumn or spring, where the plants are required and water in well, or plant individual plants in spring. Remove faded flower clusters, especially if you do not want seed to set.

Propagation Seed is available from specialist nurseries. Otherwise, you would be an unusual gardener if you did not have this plant arrive of its own accord, if it is not there already. Seed can be saved in a paper bag from the narrow, pointed seed capsules that follow the flowers. Treat as an annual, sowing seed in autumn or spring in pots or trays of compost. Seed should be scarified (the seed coat scratched) before sowing to aid germination. Plants sown in this way or ones that have self–set in the wrong place in the garden can be transplanted in spring to their required positions.

◄ **Herb Robert (*Geranium robertianum*)**

Convallaria majalis
Lily of the valley

Description

SWEET–SCENTED WHITE bellflowers adorn this rhizomatous plant in long umbels through April and May if it is given a site in which it is happy. A single stem rises from the ground with a pair of broad, tongue–shaped leaves, from between which the flower stem rises. The flowers droop from one side of this on short, fine stalks. A tough little plant, it will grow on most soils, though it is far happier in shade, even against a north–facing wall. Combines well with the bluebell, as both like shade and are strong spreaders. There are a few garden cultivars: one large-flowered variety, a pink-flowered variety and even a couple of variegated varieties, 'Albostriata' and 'Vic Pawlowski's Gold'.

How to grow

Height Up to 30cm (12in)
Habitat Woodland, usually on lime-rich or sandy soil and north-facing hedge banks.
Garden care Once established, the only jobs are to tidy up the dead flower heads and to control spread by rhizomes. It can be chopped back with a spade in autumn to the required size and the 'cuttings' either discarded or replanted.
Propagation Plants are readily available from garden centres, nurseries. Best planted between October and March. Cuttings can be taken in the form of a chunk of the plant, as described above, or as root cuttings, laid shallowly in trays of compost in autumn or early spring.

▶ **Lily of the valley (*Convallaria majalis*)**

Arum maculatum
Lords and ladies

Description

ALSO CALLED cuckoo pint, this common perennial grows from a large tuber deep in the ground. It has arrow-shaped leaves, each on an individual stalk from the base, as is the flower – or more correctly, flower spike. This appears in April and May, taking the form of a purplish spike, surrounded by a yellow–green spathe like a monk's cowl, open at one side and forming an elegant, flute-shaped bowl at the base, in which are the reproductive parts. Later, in mid to late summer, this is replaced by a tight bunch of brilliant red berries, each about the size of a pea and very toxic if eaten.

How to grow

Height Up to 50cm (20in)
Habitat Woods and shady wetlands, often on alkaline soils. Likes soil rich with organic matter.
Garden care Water in well when planting and do not let it dry out in summer. Mulch with well-rotted garden compost or manure in autumn or spring and cut down any dead stems in autumn.
Propagation Plants and seed are available from specialist nurseries. Berries can be planted in pots of compost, sealed in plastic bags and left outside over winter. Crowns can be lifted and divided in early spring every three years.

◀ **Lords and ladies (*Arum maculatum*)**

Pulmonaria officinalis
Lungwort

Description

THIS OLD garden favourite was named for its white-spotted leaves, which reminded people of lungs. The flowers are borne in panicles, some nodding, some upright. They open from red buds into sky-blue flowers, each 2.5cm (1in) or so long and tubular. The plant is semi-evergreen, the leaves dying back in summer or autumn only to reappear after a few weeks and perhaps be held all through the winter. The flowers appear from April to May and sometimes into early June. There are several cultivars sold in garden centres, but our own native is as good as any and can be found in a white-flowered form as well as several different blues. Narrow-leaved lungwort (*P. longifolia*) is found only in southern England. It has longer, slimmer leaves, often without spots.

How to grow

Height 30cm (12in)
Habitat Shady places, especially on heavy soils.
Garden care Water in well when planting and if the soil dries out in summer. Deadhead for tidiness, rather than to prolong flowering, remove dead leaves. Lift and divide plants every three years or so, as they will spread substantially.
Propagation Plants available from nurseries and garden centres. Existing plants can be lifted and divided every few years, the divisions replanted promptly and watered in well.

Carex pendula
Pendulous sedge

Description

THE LEAVES of this rhizomatous, evergreen perennial are 30–100cm (12–36in) long and up to 2cm (¾in) across, coming from reddish brown sheaths. The flower spikes, on stems that are often around 1m (3ft) tall, are long and slender. There is an orangey-red male spike at the top of the stem and from three to five yellow-flowered female spikes below it. The spikes are held one above the next along the stem, drooping away from the stem as their weight pulls it over to give the plant its characteristic stance and hence its name. The flowers are carried through May and June. Pendulous sedge is the largest of our native sedges apart from those growing in water and makes a bold and decorative garden plant, making clumps up to 60cm (24in) across.

How to grow

Height Up to 1.5m (5ft) in flower, though often only two-thirds of this height.
Habitat Damp woods and shady stream banks, often on clay soil.
Garden care Water in well when planting and ensure the ground does not dry out in summer.
Propagation Plants and seed available from some nurseries. Lift and divide clumps every three years. Seed can be sown in late summer in pots for planting out in spring.

▶ **Lungwort**
(***Pulmonaria officinalis***)

◀ **Pendulous sedge**
(***Carex pendula***)

Lysimachia nemorum
Pimpernel (yellow)

Description

MORE CLOSELY related to creeping jenny (p83) and yellow loosestrife (p87) than to the scarlet and bog pimpernels (p43 and p89), this pretty little plant is much more delicate in appearance than creeping Jenny, though it is another low, creeping perennial. The flowers, carried from May through to September, are up to 2cm (¾in) across, bright yellow and star–shaped, with five petals. The light green leaves are 4cm (1½in) long, of a rounded triangular shape with very short stalks, arising from lax, thin stems which creep among other plants or across the forest floor. The flowers are on long, slim stalks.

How to grow

Height 6cm (2½in), but spreads up to 30cm (12in).
Habitat Woodland and shady hedges, often on limestone soils, though it will thrive in pine forests. Can tolerate damp or dry soils.
Garden care Water in well when planting and again if the soil dries out in summer. Deadhead regularly to ensure a continuous supply of flowers and cut back dead stems in winter.
Propagation Plants and seed are available from specialist nurseries. Seed can be saved from existing plants. Best sown fresh in late summer or autumn, in pots left outside.

▶ **Yellow pimpernel (*Lysimachia nemorum*)**

Meconopsis cambrica
Poppy (Welsh)

Description

AS CAN be seen from the Latin name as well as from the flower itself, this plant of Wales, the West Country and the Lake District is more closely related to the blue poppies of the Himalayas than to the true poppies of the English lowlands. It will grow just about anywhere, in damp or dry conditions, in sun or shade. The flowers are yellow or orange and naturally single, though there are double varieties available as well as red ones from some sources. They are about 5cm (2in) across, born singly on 30cm (12in) stems above a clump of attractive light green feathery foliage from May until September, though the main flush is in early summer.

How to grow

Height 35cm (14in)
Habitat Usually likes dry or shady places, often on lime–rich soils. It's a good subject for the shady side of a rockery or the middle of a mixed border.
Garden care Water in well when planting, adding peat or compost to the soil. If planting in the sun, do not allow the soil to dry out too much in the summer. Deadhead regularly to prolong flowering.
Propagation Seed and plants are available from a wide range of nurseries and garden centres. Various forms are available. Seed can be sown in pots outside during late summer or early autumn.

◀ **Welsh poppy (*Meconopsis cambrica*)**

Primula vulgaris
Primrose

Description

ONCE ONE of Britain's most common and best–known wild flowers, the primrose has suffered greatly in the wild from people digging it up to take back home. Sadly, this practice was often a waste, because insufficient root was dug up with the plants and they died. However, it is thankfully far less commonly done nowadays and indeed is unnecessary because the variously coloured varieties sold commercially will often revert to the natural state after a couple of years anyway. This endlessly popular plant has long, crinkled, tongue–like leaves in a rosette which is generally flat to the ground. These are up to 20cm (8in) long, pale green, paler underneath, the undersides having a light covering of very fine hairs. The flowers are borne singly from February to May on downy stalks from the centre of the leaf rosette, opening to 4cm (1½in) wide, butter yellow with a darker yellow centre. The primrose flowers have five petals, each split at the tip, and deep-set central reproductive parts, some with the stamens prominent, others with the female style more obvious. There are numerous commercially grown varieties of primrose, and the plant is available in many different colours, ranging from white to rich reds and blues, some with the central dark yellow eye, some without. Also, several double–flowered varieties of primrose have been bred for garden use.

How to grow

Height Flowers up to 15cm (6in) high.
Habitat Found in woodland, hedge bottoms and short–cut pasture. Often grows in shade, which seems to promote stronger growth and tends to prefer heavy or limy soils.
Garden care Water in well when planting. Deadhead regularly to prolong flowering. If not allowed to set seed, plants will regroup and flower again later in the summer. They can be in flower as early as Christmas and kept going on and off until August.
Propagation Plants are available from just about anywhere you can think of to buy them. Seed can be obtained from garden centres and nurseries. Existing plants can be allowed to self–seed, then the young plants dug up and moved to the desired position, or seed can be saved and sown in pots or trays outside in summer. The seed needs a period of cold before it will germinate, so be patient if sowing in pots and do not keep them in the greenhouse.

◀ **Primrose (*Primula vulgaris*)**

Allium ursinum
Ramsons

Description

A MEMBER OF the onion family, along with the decorative alliums often used in gardens, this strongly aromatic bulbous perennial is also called wild garlic and has been used for the same purposes as that plant, which is also a close relative. Ramsons usually grows in large colonies in the wild, so that the strong smell will be noticed sometimes before the starry white flowers in spring and early summer. The leaves are long–stalked and broadly strap–like, similar to those of lily of the valley (p145); the flowers are borne in spherical bunches on long stalks separate to those of the leaves. Looks lovely with bluebell (p140) and red campion (p59).

How to grow

Height 15–35cm (6–14in)
Habitat Deciduous woodland and hedge bottoms, often on damp ground.
Garden care Although it looks pretty, it does not smell so and is better at the far end of the garden. Bulbs should be planted in autumn and kept watered throughout the summer, after flowering is over. Dead stems and leaves can be cut away in late summer and a mulch of well–rotted garden compost applied after this.
Propagation Bulbs are available from some nurseries and occasionally in garden centres. Clumps can be lifted and divided every three years or so.

▶ **Ramsons**
(*Allium ursinum*)

Galanthus nivalis
Snowdrop

Description

L IKE THE primrose and the bluebell, this lovely little plant is not as common as it once was in the wild, because people used to go out and dig them up for the garden. The flowers are borne singly on slender stalks, the leaves narrow and greyish–green, up to 15cm (6in) long, rising from small, brown bulbs, just beneath the surface of the earth. In some sheltered parts of the south–east of England, they are open in time for Christmas, though more usually it is January or February before the three outer petals and three shorter inner ones open to herald the beginning of spring. There are dozens of garden cultivars, many actually bred from the closely related *G. elwesii*, from Europe. They include giant ones, double ones, dwarf ones and countless others.

How to grow

Height 7.5–15cm (3–6in)
Habitat Open woods and copses, where it will enjoy part sun and part shade, with plenty of organic matter to feed the bulbs.
Garden care Plant in the green, that is with the leaves still growing. Mulch in March, after the flowers have finished, with leaf mould or compost. Transplant bulbs in February or March, after flowers have finished, but while leaves are still green.
Propagation Available from garden centres and nurseries. Will spread and can be divided in spring.

◀ **Snowdrop**
(*Galanthus nivalis*)

Polygonatum multiflorum
Solomon's seal

Description

UNUSUALLY, THIS plant is named for its roots, which were said in ancient times to resemble the seal of Solomon, otherwise known as the Star of David. The stems are long and unbranched, often with several to a plant and the leaves arranged along the upper half to two-thirds in twin rows, standing out horizontally or semi-upright, each one broadly elliptical in shape. In May and June clusters of narrow, white, bell-shaped flowers, each 2cm (¾in) long, hang beneath the stems. These develop later into blue-black berries. There are several closely related species native to Britain. The plant usually sold in garden centres is a cross between *P. multiflorum* and angular Solomon's seal (*P. odoratum*), which has an angled stem and usually solitary flowers. This species is found in more open, drier places, such as rocky outcrops, dry grassland and woodland clearings.

How to grow

Height About 60cm (24in)
Habitat A woodland plant, it will thrive in most soil types, but benefits from having peat or compost added to the soil. Likes shade or partial shade.
Garden care Mulch in autumn and again in spring, water in dry spells and keep a watch in summer for sawfly caterpillars, which can strip the leaves in a few days if left unchecked.
Propagation Available from nurseries and garden centres. Lift and divide clumps every few years, replanting the young, outer sections where needed.

▶ **Solomon's seal**
(*Polygonatum multiflorum*)

Oxalis acetosella
Sorrel (wood)

Description

THERE ARE several species of *oxalis*, this being one of two that are native to Britain: the other has tiny brownish leaves and even tinier yellow flowers in summer, spreading to form a low mat of foliage between rocks and stones, often in shady areas. Generally, the non-native species are sun-lovers, their flowers pink or red and 2.5cm (1in) across. All have five petals and clover-like trifoliate leaves. The wood sorrel is a rhizomatous perennial which used to be common in woods throughout Britain, though it is less so now. It has slender, pinkish stems, leaves and flowers being borne individually on stems up to 12cm (5in) long. The delicate white flowers, up to 2.5cm (1in) across and sometimes veined lilac or purple, appear in April and May and close up at sunset. The leaves are a pale, yellowish green.

How to grow

Height Up to 12cm (5in), though often smaller
Habitat Likes woodland, often in damp places but sometimes among rocks. Thrives best in shade.
Garden care Dig in some compost when planting, water in well; afterwards if the stems begin to droop. Cut away old leaves in autumn.

Propagation Seed and plants available from specialist nurseries. Plants can be dug up and divided in spring.

◀ **Wood sorrel**
(*Oxalis acetosella*)

Helleborus foetidus
Stinking hellebore

Description

ONE OF several hellebores grown in gardens, including the Christmas rose (*H. niger*) and the lenten rose (*H. orientalis*), this one is actually a native. It has a thick, branched, pale–green stem and long–stemmed, dark–green leaves, each made up of anything from three to nine narrow strap–like leaflets, arranged in a fan–like design. These can be anything up to 15cm (6in) long. The flowers are borne in panicles at the tops of the stems. Each flower is up to 2.5cm (1in) across, drooping and bell–shaped or globular with purple edges to the yellow–green petals. The stinking hellebore flowers from late February to the end of April or even into May. The other native hellebore, the green hellebore (*H. viridis*), is shorter and has wide–open green flowers.

How to grow

Height Up to 75cm (30in), though often smaller.
Habitat Likes dry slopes, scrub and woodland, often on lime–rich soil. Very shade–tolerant, but it can take the sun for at least part of the day.
Garden care Water in well when planting, deadhead after flowering has finished, unless seed is required. Plants can suffer from rust; affected leaves should be removed.
Propagation Plants and seed are available from nurseries and garden centres, especially in early spring. Seed can be saved and sown in pots or allowed to self-seed. Plants can be divided every three years.

▶ **Stinking hellebore (*Helleborus foetidus*)**

Stellaria holostea
Stitchwort (greater)

Description

THIS PRETTY, delicate–looking perennial flowers abundantly in spring. The flowers are up to 2.5cm (1in) across, each of the five white petals being divided almost into two down the centre. It looks stunning with bluebell (p140) and red campion (p59). There are two other stitchworts native to Britain. Lesser stitchwort (*S. graminea*) is a smaller, finer plant of heath and dry grassland, with paler green stems and leaves and smaller flowers in May. Bog stitchwort (*S. alsine*) has smaller flowers again, the green sepals between the petals being longer than the petals and open from May to July. Similar, but difficult to obtain, is the field mousear (*Cerastium arvense*).

How to grow

Height Up to 60cm (24in)
Habitat Grows in woodland and hedgerows. Tolerates shade.
Garden care Plant in groups and give the support of close association with other plants and you will get a starry white display for several weeks. Cut down the stems in late summer after seed has set, or deadhead if seeding is not required.
Propagation Seed is available from a few specialist nurseries, but it is worth the search. Sow in pots or trays in late summer or early autumn and leave outside to germinate, then plant out.

▼ **Greater stitchwort (*Stellaria holostea*)**

Viola riviniana
Violet (common dog)

Description

THIS IS the most common of the ten species that grow wild in Britain, many of which are difficult to tell apart. It is a small perennial which has a rosette of dark green, heart–shaped leaves, usually hairless and finely toothed at the edges, about 2.5cm (1in) long on long stalks. The flowers are on even longer stalks, arising from the leaf nodes. They are scentless, violet–purple and about 2.5cm (1in) across. Often there are dark lines near the centre of the flower. The flowers have five petals. The common dog violet flowers from early March into June. Generally, the violets are invaluable plants for spring colour in a range of situations, from damp shade to dry rocks.

How to grow

Height Up to 20cm (8in)
Habitat Found on grassland and woodland floors, also among rocks. Happy in sun or shade, but does not appreciate very acid soils or wetness.
Garden care Very little is needed. Deadheading will prolong flowering to some extent, but otherwise the plants can be left to their own devices once planted. They will happily self–seed around the garden if allowed to do so, but not in an invasive manner.
Propagation Plants and seed are available from nurseries. Seed can be saved and plants can be dug up and divided every few years. Cuttings can be taken in summer and potted up in coarse compost.

▶ **Common dog violet (*Viola riviniana*)**

Galium odoratum
Woodruff

Description

SOMETIMES CALLED sweet woodruff for the smell of new–mown hay which it exudes when dried, this slender perennial is a member of the bedstraw family. Its narrow, pointed leaves are up to 5cm (2in) long and are carried in whorls of six to nine around the stem. The flowers are tiny, white funnels, opening to four petals at the top, and are borne in broad bunches at the tops of long stalks during April and May. A very pretty plant when found in a clump in a spring woodland, it has a delicate look lacking in some of the other spring flowers.

How to grow

Height Up to 30cm (12in)
Habitat A woodland plant found in neutral or alkaline soils, often in beech woods. Can tolerate deep or partial shade or some sun.
Garden care Water it in well when planting, deadhead when the flowers are over and cut back in late autumn.
Propagation Available from specialist nurseries as seed or plants, the seed can be saved from existing plants and sown in pots outside in summer or a head of flowers can be left on the plant and allowed to self–seed.

Woodruff (*Galium odoratum*)

Carex sylvatica
Wood sedge

Description

THIS DENSELY tufted, evergreen perennial grows from short rhizomes. The soft, bright, yellowish-green leaves can be up to 60cm (2ft) long, but are more often about half that or even much less, depending on the growing conditions. It is a tolerant plant, growing in sun or shade, on damp or dry soil. The arching tufts are very decorative with or without the flowering stems, which appear from mid–May to July and can be up to 60cm (2ft) tall, thin and arching, with a group of three male flower heads at the tip and female heads born further down the stem.

How to grow

Height Anything from 10–60cm (4–24in)
Habitat Usually found in woods, on clay or chalk, often on damp ground or open moorland. It can also tolerate dry conditions.
Garden care Preferably provide some organic matter when planting and water in well. Remove dead leaves and stems to prevent pests.
Propagation Plants and seed are available from some garden centres and nurseries. Plants can be lifted and divided every three years. Flower heads can be bent down and pegged to the ground once seed has set. Shaking the head and then giving it a light covering of compost should dislodge the seeds and begin the process of germination.

▶ **Wood sedge
(Carex sylvatica)**

Lamiastrum galeobdolon
Yellow archangel

Description

LOOKING LIKE a nettle, especially when not in flower, this square-stalked perennial with opposite pairs of toothed leaves, lacking the indented bases of some of its less amenable close relatives, is becoming rare in the wild. It is popular with gardeners, especially the variegated 'Florentinum' and one or two less keenly spreading varieties such as 'Silver Carpet'. A close relative of the white dead nettle (*Lamium album*), it has whorls of large, nettle-like, yellow flowers in the axils of the upper leaves from April to July. The flowering stems rise from creeping stems that spread quite widely. It looks good in spring with bluebells (p140) and stitchwort (p151) in a shady spot.

How to grow

Height Up to 60cm (24in), but often 25cm (10in).
Habitat Deciduous woodland and shady banks, especially on lime-rich soils.
Garden care Water in well when planting. Deadhead regularly to extend the flowering season and to prevent self-seeding.
Propagation Seed and plants are available from nurseries and some garden centres. Seed can be saved and plants divided every few years. Seed should be sown in spring or summer where it is to flower, or in pots or trays outside to be planted out in the autumn or early in the following spring. The seed needs a period of cold before it will germinate.

▲ **Yellow archangel (*Lamiastrum galeobdolon*)**

There are a whole host of things that make a garden feel like part of a home, but one of the essentials has to be birdsong, as attested by the thousands of bird tables, nest boxes and bird baths sold every year. It is the trees and climbers that attract birds into our gardens, giving them places to perch, to roost and to nest as well as often to feed. Although you need to choose carefully, you'll find trees and climbers offer a whole new dimension to your garden.

Trees and climbers

Growing trees and climbers

ALTHOUGH ALMOST every garden has its share of climbers, including native ones, many people are cautious of using trees in their gardens nowadays. Architects use them in giving overall plans to modern estates and in giving new office complexes, which are often built in ultra–modern style, a natural element, but we seem to have something of an aversion to placing something of such scale in our gardens. This is difficult to understand because trees do so much more than offer shade. They give a sense of scale to the buildings as well as to the garden itself. They provide intimacy in ways that shrubs, hedges, fences and climbers cannot. Trees help to enclose a garden, define its space and give shelter from that great expanse of blue above, making a garden feel more like an outside room, rather than a broad, open expanse. And beyond all that, they can provide interest in the garden through most – and in some cases all – of the seasons with attractive bark, blossom, leaves and berries.

How to plant trees

TREES ARE available either as pot–grown specimens or bare–rooted in autumn and winter. Pot-grown trees can be planted at any time of year as long as the ground is not frozen, but for the first year they should be watered well, and will require staking. There are a number of methods of staking, but perhaps the best is to use a stake set at around forty–five degrees into the ground, crossing the trunk about 30 to 60cm (12–24in) above ground level. Tie this to the tree with a plastic tie, which should be checked regularly and loosened off if it begins to cut into the bark. Young trees will also need protecting from rabbits and other wild animals which might damage the bark or strip the foliage. Protective plastic spirals are not the most attractive appliances, but they are invaluable if there is any risk that herbivores will gain

▼ **Summer-flowering climbers.**

Dog rose   Jack-by-the-hedge   Honeysuckle

Buying trees

When you buy a tree, do not buy just one, for it will look odd and lonely; instead, buy two or three, either of the same type or contrasting ones. Make sure you choose healthy, well-proportioned specimens.

access to the trees. Whether they are pot-grown or bare-rooted, trees need careful planting. Use a planting hole at least twice the size you think is required! With a bare-rooted specimen, spread the roots out comfortably across the hole and feed soil in between, packing it in tightly to leave the junction between roots and trunk at exactly

ground level. A useful way to judge this is to lay a piece of wood across the planting hole, so that its centre passes beside the tree.

Pot-grown trees also need a large planting hole, which can be refilled with a mixture of natural soil and a compost medium that is similar to that in the pot. If the roots are looking at all constricted when the pot is removed, tease them out around the edges of the root ball to encourage them to spread out.

The root systems of pot-grown trees will not be as sturdy and well-developed as for bare-root ones, so will need more care in their first year in the garden. But pot-grown specimens will generally provide a more immediate effect in the garden. However, bare-root specimens tend to establish better, as long as they are soaked well before planting and kept watered until they

▼ **Tree blossom in late spring.**

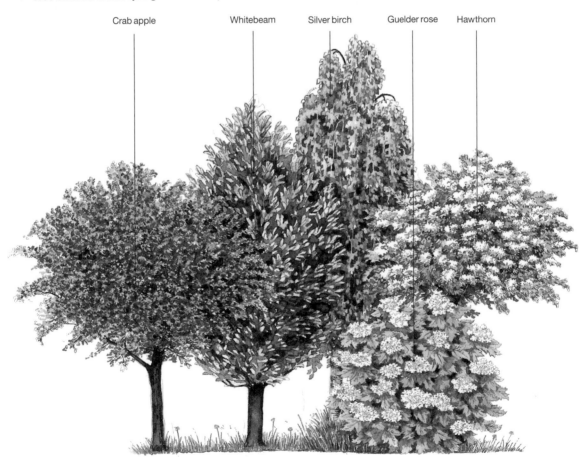

Crab apple   Whitebeam   Silver birch   Guelder rose   Hawthorn

are established. Ideally, with either pot–grown or bare–root trees, you should leave a slight depression around the root–ball once planting is completed. This allows water to be concentrated into where it is needed when watering.

Plant choice: trees

Among Britain's native trees, of which there are over 30, there are many very decorative species and varieties. Some are small, barely more than bushes, and others huge, up to well

Get inspired

Before you make your choice, why not go and visit some of the most beautiful places in Britain for inspiration. Parks, arboretums, forests and woods will all provide that much-needed preview of what you can expect when your own trees mature.

▼ **Trees and climbers used for autumn colour.**

Silver birch   Ivy   Ferns   Periwinkle   Rowan

over 33m (100ft) tall, such as the Scots pine (*Pinus sylvestris*) or the common oak (p167). These, of course, are not for the average suburban garden, though they are certainly handsome plants and are worthy of use where there is space.

Aside from the evergreens like the Scots pine, yew (p171), holly (p127) and ivy (p166), the beech (p161) and hornbeam (p165) retain their leaves, albeit dead and brown, through most of the winter. In the earliest weeks of spring or even before, the cherry plum (p162) and the blackthorn (p120) come into flower, followed closely by the bright new leaf buds of the hawthorn (p125) and the poplars. Many trees come into flower and into leaf as spring progresses and turns into summer, then the berries take over, providing bright splashes of red, yellow, purple and orange that are supported or even supplanted by the rich autumn leaf colour of deciduous species like field maple (p164), willows and cherries. Even before this, through the spring and summer, leaf colour is an important element with our native trees. The cherry plum and the beech both come in green- or bronze-leaved forms. The whitebeam (p170) and white willow (*Salix alba*) both have silvery foliage while the lime (p166) provides a bright, fresh green that is hard to beat through the height of summer.

Tree size

Trees do not need to be enormous or overpowering in the garden. Many can be grown perfectly well in containers and can flourish this way for decades. One can keep a tree pruned to whatever size is required. Some of our native trees even make ideal bonsai specimens. Hawthorn, Scots pine and oak (p165) are all perfect for this type of culture with their naturally gnarled and twisting growth habits.

Plant choice: climbers

WE HAVE over a dozen native climbers, too, and innumerable cultivated varieties of some of them, such as ivy and honeysuckle (p164). These can clothe walls, fences, pergolas and arches as well as free-standing obelisks or shrubs that have a short season of interest. Some are evergreen, others not. Indeed, though they reach a height of several metres some are herbaceous, dying back to ground level each winter. The everlasting sweet pea (p169) and the hop (p165) are common examples of this latter group. And climbers are not always used in the vertical. Ivy is often employed to drape the sides of containers. Everlasting sweet peas and tufted vetch (p169) are commonly used to scramble through and between other plants in a mixed border, adding late colour where other plants have given of their best earlier in the year and, on a larger scale, old man's beard (p168) does exactly the same, clothing hedges and shrubs with a soft and feathery mass of silver seed heads through the winter months.

Propagation

LIKE THE shrubs, trees produce fruit or berries and, if you do not need instant impact in the garden, it can be fun to collect and plant the seed. In the same way as for shrubs, berries can be picked and placed in layers in a pot, alternating with moist compost before covering the whole thing, labelling it and burying it over winter in the garden to allow the hard coating on the seeds to soften before sowing in spring. This can be an enjoyable way of introducing children to gardening too. Their sense of wonder as a tiny seedling breaks the surface of the soil and begins to grow into something that may end up a hundred feet tall can be magical.

Alnus glutinosa
Alder

Description

OFTEN SEEN growing with willows, the alder is a moisture–loving tree. The long, yellow male catkins appear at the same time as the rounded, dark brown, cone–like female ones in February or March. The leaves are held alternately on long stalks from the pale grey twigs and are quite round, with finely toothed edges and a well–defined indentation in the tip. Decorative cut-leaved varieties have been bred for garden and park use. Alder can be pollarded and the young shoots will have a purplish colour which contrasts well with the yellow twigs of some of the willows or certain varieties of dogwood (p122).

How to grow

Height A fair–sized tree, the alder can attain 12m (40ft) or more.
Habitat Likes damp soil and plenty of light, but can be found in drier places and in shady oak woods.
Garden care Plant in damp or wet ground and if a full sized tree is not what you require, then pollard it or coppice it every three years after the first five.
Propagation Plants are available from nurseries, both in natural and cut-leaved forms. Semi–ripe cuttings can be taken in summer, cutting to just below a leaf node and planting in a sheltered spot in the ground.

▶ Alder (*Alnus glutinosa*)

Fraxinus excelsior
Ash (common)

Description

THE COMMON ash is easily identified in any season. Its bark is pale grey and only lightly fissured. The buds of both leaves and flowers are black, pointed ovals and can be found on the twigs at any time of year. The seeds are in the form of 'keys' – that is, each seed is individually held on a stalk and has a slender, papery wing attached to it. The leaves themselves are divided like those of the rowan (p168) and are the last to appear in late spring, often into late May. There is a weeping variety called 'Pendula' and a range of varieties with decoratively coloured leaves.

How to grow

Height Usually up to 18m (60ft), though it can approach twice that in ideal conditions.
Habitat Edges of flowing water or fresh lakes, woodland, in hedgerows or dry slopes.
Garden care A tough tree, the ash suffers very little from pests and diseases, though it does have one downside: it suckers freely so these need to be pulled off from the point of origin on the root. Water in well when planting and stake low down to allow a good root system to develop.
Propagation Saplings are available from nurseries. Hardwood cuttings can be taken in late summer and rooted in a sheltered spot in the garden. The seeds germinate freely in the garden or in pots of compost.

◀ **Common ash**
(*Fraxinus excelsior*)

Fagus sylvatica
Beech (common)

Description

THIS MAGNIFICENT tree is not one for small gardens unless it is being used as a hedge, to which it adapts very successfully. Its leaves are held alternately along the somewhat zigzagging stem and are bright green on both sides, unless the highly decorative copper beech ('Purpurea') is used, when they are a deep, mahogany bronze colour. In late autumn they turn a rich orange and are held on the branches well into the winter, especially if it is mild. The bark of the beech is smooth and usually grey.

How to grow

Height Grows up to 33m (108ft) as a mature tree. As a hedging shrub, it can be kept to 2m (6ft) high quite comfortably.
Habitat Prefers deep soil, loam or chalk. Often found on hills, where the soil is dry.
Garden care Firm in and water well when planting. Few pests or diseases will trouble it. If using it for a hedge, it can be clipped twice a year to keep it to size, however wait until the hedge is about 15cm (6in) taller than needed.
Propagation Usually sold in autumn and winter as bare–rooted plants. Available from nurseries and garden centres. Hardwood cuttings can be taken in late summer and rooted in the garden, but they are best left until the following autumn for transplanting, after the leaves have changed.

▶ **Common beech**
(*Fagus sylvatica*)

Prunus padus
Cherry (bird)

Description

NAMED BECAUSE its black fruit are edible only by birds, this tree is a spectacular sight in April or May, when its shiny, dark brown branches are festooned with long racemes of white blossom while the leaves are still young. The leaves are roughly ovate, with a definite point to the tip and fine serration along the edges. Both the flowers and the leaves give off a smell of bitter almond. The branches of the tree form an attractive conical shape. There are several cultivars including forms with pink flowers, double flowers and a spectacular one with huge hanging spikes of creamy flowers called 'Waterei'.

How to grow

Height Up to 10m (30ft)
Habitat Woods, scrub and hedgerows.
Garden care Can take full sun or shade of larger trees. Prone to attack by red spider mite, aphids, brown rot, silver leaf and cherry bacterial banker, so a spray should be used as soon as problems are seen. Discard all affected material immediately. Pruning in the warmest months of the year will lessen the chances of silver leaf attack.
Propagation Plants are available from nurseries and some garden centres. Hardwood cuttings can be taken in summer and heeled in a shady spot to shoot by next spring.

◀ **Bird cherry**
(*Prunus padus*)

Prunus cerasifera
Cherry plum

Description

CHERRY PLUMS flower with blackthorn (p120) in February and March, opening stalked white blossoms with their prominent reddish anthers before leaves emerge from their buds. With its smooth, dark bark, it resembles the blackthorn though its foliage is thinner and the leaves larger. It bears cherry–like fruit on short stalks in bunches along the twigs in late summer and autumn, before the leaves turn yellow and fall. The best–known form of the cherry plum is probably the purple–leaved 'Atropurpurea' or 'Pissardii' variety, which has pale–pink blossom.

How to grow

Height Up to 8m (24ft) as a tree, though it can be cut and used as a hedge of 2m (6ft) high.
Habitat Most often seen in hedgerows, it can also be found in woodland on normal to dry soils.
Garden care Can be attacked by cherry bacterial canker and silver leaf. Affected branches must be cut off, destroyed and the wound dressed. Brown rot mainly affects the fruit, but can also get into the leaves and wood, and requires pruning out.
Propagation Plants are available from nurseries and garden centres. The fruit can be gathered and sown in pots of compost in autumn, left outside to germinate over winter. Hardwood cuttings can be taken in autumn and rooted in a shady place.

▼ Cherry plum (***Prunus cerasifera***)

Prunus avium
Cherry (wild)

Description

ALSO CALLED the gean, the wild cherry is the parent of edible cherry trees and is still used as the grafting rootstock for them. Though each tree flowers for only two or three weeks, the display is worth growing the tree for on its own, even without the shiny, chestnut–brown bark with its thin horizontal cracks, the small fruits in mid summer and the fiery blaze of crimson as the leaves turn in autumn. The tree is generally conical in shape. Its leaves are elliptical and sharply pointed at the tips, the margins toothed. The wild cherry tree is a fast grower, though not large. The tree will need to be netted if you are to beat the birds to the cherries.

How to grow

Height Up to 13m (45ft), though often less
Habitat Naturally found in woods and occasionally hedgerows, usually on chalk or limestone soils. Tolerates shade well, though it is equally happy in the sun.
Garden care Water in well when planting and use a low stake. See the 'Garden care' section of cherry plum for details of diseases.
Propagation Saplings are available from nurseries and some garden centres. Semi–ripe cuttings can be taken in summer and rooted in a sheltered spot in the garden or fruit can be potted up in compost kept damp by sealing in a plastic bag until germination.

◄ Wild cherry (***Prunus avium***)

Malus sylvestris
Crab apple

Description

RELATED TO the roses, this small tree has spines along its grey–brown twigs. These have obviously been bred out in the process of producing the cultivated apples, of which this is the main, or perhaps the sole, parent. The leaves are also reminiscent of the rose family, being ovate with serrated edges. They are a mid green in colour, opening in April from reddish, hairy buds and turning a bright yellow in autumn. The blossom follows the leaves in late April and is borne in small bunches above the leaves; the five petals usually white with a pinkish tinge to the backs. The fruit, 4cm (1½in) across, is a miniature yellowish apple, sometimes with a hint of red to the skin. They are hard and bitter, but used for crab apple jelly as well as jam and wine. There are several garden cultivars of the crab apple, grown for their ornamental value. Most are at least partly derived from Asian or North American parentage. They include some varieties with purple leaves, red or pink flowers, ones with red buds that open to white flowers and several different fruit colours.

diseases are best dealt with by removing infected tissue and destroying it. However, if the tree is in good condition, this will make it less prone to most problems in the first place. Give the tree space for the air to flow around it. Feed it once a year if the soil is not particularly fertile. Water it if there is a prolonged dry spell, especially if it is being grown in close association with other plants, including grass. Prune out old or crossing branches from the centre of the tree, remembering to cut right back to the joint and make the cut as flush as possible with the surrounding wood. Pruning is best done in summer, when the tree is actively growing and so will heal more quickly.

Propagation Plants are available from nurseries and garden centres. If you already have one, or have access to one, you can plant the seed yourself, but it will be a long time before you have a significant garden tree.

▼ Crab apple (*Malus sylvestris*)

How to grow

Height Up to 10m (30ft), but often smaller and can be kept in check by pruning out the long growing shoots.
Habitat Naturally found in hedgerows and woods, it is happy in dry to normal soil conditions, sun or shade.
Garden care Apples, whether wild or cultivated, are prone to a number of diseases and different pests. These are best dealt with as soon as they are noticed, so that they do not weaken the tree. There are several relatively eco–friendly insecticides on the market now to deal with pests. Fungal, viral and bacterial

Acer campestre
Field maple

Description

THIS NATIVE acer is much smaller than the other two species that grow wild in Britain, the sycamore (*A. pseudoplatanus*) and the Norway maple (*A. platanoides*). All have distinctly acer-like divided palmate leaves, but those of the field maple have rounded, rather than pointed, tips to the lobes. The field maple makes a good hedgerow plant as well as a very attractive tree, if allowed to mature. In spring the yellow flowers are borne in loose clusters as the orangey–pink leaves emerge, so that the whole tree blazes orange in the sunshine. The mature leaves are a fresh, bright green, turning to amber in autumn.

How to grow

Height Up to 18m (60ft), though it rarely gets to more than half that. It can be cut regularly to make a bush or hedge, best kept to about 2m (6ft).
Habitat Prefers well-drained soil and full sun.
Garden care The acers can be prone to disease. Tar spot is a leaf fungus, producing black marks, on the undersides of the leaves. Galls, rust and black spot can also affect the leaves. All can be pruned out and the affected parts destroyed.
Propagation Young trees are available from nurseries. The seeds will freely germinate, though they are less of a nuisance than those of the sycamore. Hardwood cuttings can be taken in late summer and rooted over winter in a sheltered spot.

▶ **Field maple (Acer campestre)**

Lonicera periclymenum
Honeysuckle

Description

ALSO KNOWN as woodbine, this excellent climber flowers between June and September. It has cream flowers tinged with yellow and pink, borne in clusters of six or more. These are highly scented and full of nectar and are followed by clusters of unpalatable bright red berries. The woody stems climb by twisting clockwise around whatever support is available. The plant is deciduous, with small, soft green leaves along the stem.

How to grow

Height Up to 6m (20ft)
Habitat Widespread in hedgerows and woodland. Well known for its tolerance of shade.
Garden care Provide firm support. Tie in when young and prune as space dictates in spring. Can be prone to black spot and mildew. Proprietary sprays can be used for these. Best planted near to the house, where the gorgeous, rich evening scent can be enjoyed to the full.
Propagation From seed or cuttings or as plants from a garden centre or nursery. Cuttings can be rooted in well-drained compost with no need for rooting powder, or in a jar of water.

◀ **Honeysuckle (Lonicera periclymenum)**

Humulus lupulus
Hops

Description

THIS HERBACEOUS perennial climber is useful in the garden for decorative purposes. Several thin twining stems arise from the overwintered rootstock in spring, twisting up whatever support is available as they grow, rapidly putting out a profusion of large, jagged–edged leaves with three broad lobes. The male plants have starry yellow flowers in July and August. The female flowers are tiny and green though it is these that will later develop into the cone–like fruits used in brewing. Often used in the garden is the golden hop ('Aurea'), which has rich yellowish leaves, especially when grown in full sun.

How to grow

Height Up to 5m (15ft), though it dies back to ground level at the end of each year.
Habitat Probably originally a plant of damp woodland, it can tolerate sun or shade, wet or dry soil, but is usually found on neutral to alkaline ground, such as the chalk of Kent and Sussex.
Garden care Dig in organic matter when planting and mulch with well–rotted manure each year. Chop back runners from the roots or dig them up and pot them if new plants are required. Cut away dead stems at the end of each year.
Propagation Plants and seeds are available from garden centres and nurseries. Plants can be lifted and divided every few years. If you have a female plant, seed can be saved and sown in spring or autumn.

▶ **Hops (*Humulus lupulus*)**

Carpinus betulus
Hornbeam

Description

ONE OF the more useful of our native trees, the hornbeam is also very decorative. Its name derives from the Old English words for 'hard' and 'tree' and the wood is still used for butcher's blocks, skittles and mallets. The tree can become quite large if conditions allow, but is also commonly used for hedging, when it will form a dense, neat growth which has the advantage over beech (*Fagus sylvatica*) that it will retain some of its dead leaves through the winter. Its leaves look a little like those of beech, but are toothed like those of the elms.

How to grow

Height Up to 26m (85ft), but often coppiced, pollarded or used for hedging.
Habitat Naturally found in beech and oak woods, where it can tolerate deep shade. Grows well on most soil types, including chalk, but is best on clay, in sun or shade.
Garden care Water in well when planting. If growing a hedge, clip annually in July.
Propagation Available from garden centres and nurseries. In late autumn and winter, sold as bare-rooted saplings. Seed can be saved from existing trees and sown outdoors in autumn, the seedlings transplanted in the following spring.

◀ **Hornbeam (*Carpinus betulus*)**

Hedera helix
Ivy

Description

THERE ARE countless varieties of ivy for sale throughout the country. Some are green-leaved, some yellow-variegated, some silver-variegated; some large, some dwarf. Ivies are evergreen and, perversely, they flower in the autumn and produce berries in the spring. The flowers are small, greenish-yellow and fairly insignificant, though sweet scented. The berries are held in tight clumps and ripen to a purplish-black colour. It can make an excellent wall-cover on its own or act as a contrasting background for other climbers, such as clematis or hops (p165).

How to grow

Height The wild species can grow to almost 33m (100ft), but cultivated varieties can be as small as 30cm (12in) long at maturity.
Habitat Will climb over any support, be it a wall, a tree stump or a living tree. Grows in sun or shade, often on the driest of soils.
Garden care Water in well when planting, firming the soil around the roots, train in the required direction. The waxy leaves repel just about any pest or disease attack.
Propagation Plants are freely available in just about any outlet. Cuttings can be taken in the warmer months and potted up, the pots sealed in plastic bags until rooting has occurred and the cuttings begin to grow.

▶ **Ivy**
(*Hedera helix*)

Tilia x europaea
Lime (common)

Description

POTENTIALLY THE tallest of Britain's broad-leaved trees, the common lime is a hybrid between two native species of lime, the large-leaved lime (*T. platyphyllus*) and the small-leaved lime (*T. cordata*), neither of which is now common. The common lime is a lovely tree, roughly pyramidal in overall shape, the dark-grey trunk straight and upright. The leaves are broad and almost heart-shaped, up to 10cm (4in) long and bright green. The tree flowers in early July, when the bright yellow, sweetly scented flowers are held in small bunches at the tips of the twigs.

How to grow

Height Potentially up to 43m (140ft) in deep, loamy soil, though it averages around 23m (75ft).
Habitat Limes like deep soil with plenty of nutrients, such as is often found in river valleys in lowland areas. They need good air flow around the leaves.
Garden care Air pollution in towns renders the lime prone to attack by aphids, which cause it to drip sap on to the ground beneath. A black mould then grows on this, while the tops of the leaves can develop orangey nail galls.
Propagation Young trees are available from nurseries. Semi-ripe cuttings can be taken in summer and rooted in a sheltered spot in the garden, to be transplanted the following spring.

◀ **Common lime**
(*Tilia x europaea*)

Solanum dulcamara
Nightshade (woody)

Description

ALSO KNOWN as bittersweet, this relative of the potato and tomato bears smooth, heart–shaped leaves on long stalks from the thin, dark, twining stems. The main stem is woody at the base, as opposed to that of the black nightshade (*S. nigra*), which has black stems and white flowers, and dies back in winter. The flowers of the woody nightshade are about 1cm (½in) long and purple and yellow in colour. They are carried in branched bunches, just two or three of which will be open at any time. The berries, along with the rest of the plant, are poisonous. So too are the black nightshade (*S. nigrum*) and the deadly nightshade (*Atropa belladona*), which is a medium–sized herbaceous plant, not a climber like the others.

How to grow

Height Up to 2.1m (7ft)

Habitat Grows in sun or shade, in damp or dry soil. Readily found in hedges or on dry slopes, in wet woodland or on shingle beaches.

Garden care Plant close to some support. Do not plant if small children are going to use the garden, as the berries are toxic, if not deadly.

Propagation Available from some nurseries. Berries can be picked and potted outside in autumn to germinate in spring, after the cold has broken their dormancy.

▼ **Woody nightshade (*Solanum dulcamara*)**

Quercus robur
Oak (English)

Description

THE GNARLED and twisted dark reddish–brown branches of the English oak clothed in leaves is an essentially British sight. The English oak is one of many species worldwide and one of two native to the British Isles. The other is the much straighter and more upright sessile oak (*Q. petraea*). The term 'sessile' refers to the fact that the acorns of this tree are unstalked, unlike its close relative. The bark of this tree is also much paler, though similar in texture, being finely cracked and vertically ridged. Both trees are large, eventually achieving 33m (100ft) or more, so are suited only to large gardens and parklands.

How to grow

Height Up to 40m (120ft), but it grows slowly.

Habitat At home on most soils, it is less common on chalk and limestone.

Garden care This tough tree needs little care. The main disease of the oak is the oak–apple or gall, a growth formed in response to a parasitic wasp. Prune out affected shoots as soon as they are found and burn or remove from the site.

Propagation Saplings are available from nurseries, usually as pot–grown plants. Semi–ripe cuttings can be taken with a heel and potted up after dipping into hormone rooting powder, or the acorns can be planted in pots and the seedlings planted out.

◄ **English oak (*Quercus robur*)**

Clematis vitalba
Old man's beard

Description

ALSO KNOWN as wild clematis, or traveller's joy for the frothy abundance of its seed heads through autumn and winter, old man's beard is a climbing shrub common in hedgerows in southern Britain, especially on chalk and limestone. It climbs over other shrubs and trees by means of twisting, clinging leaf-stalks, the leaves divided into three lobes, each dark green and heart-shaped. White-petalled flowers with a mass of stamens are about 2.5cm (1in) across and are borne from late June into September. From October onwards its seeds are displayed in little balls of white hair 4cm (1½in) across.

How to grow

Height Up to 10m (30ft)
Habitat Hedgerows and woodland edges, usually on lime or chalk soils, in sun or partial shade.
Garden care Plant deep, to encourage shooting and to avoid clematis wilt disease. Treat grey mould or black spot on the leaves by removing affected leaves or with a proprietary fungicide. Pruning is best done in February, cutting back hard to within a foot of the ground.
Propagation Plants and seed are available from specialist nurseries. Seed can be sown in autumn or spring. Cuttings can be taken in June. They root from internodal cuttings so the basal cut should be made about halfway between leaf nodes, rather than just beneath one.

▶ **Old man's beard**
(*Clematis vitalba*)

Sorbus aucuparia
Rowan

Description

ALSO KNOWN as the mountain ash, for the superficial resemblance of its leaves to those of the ash (p160), this tough, hardy tree is often seen in mountainous regions, sometimes clinging to the most precarious positions on scree slopes or almost vertical rock faces. The pale green, feathery foliage appears in April and is followed in May or June by the broad, flattened heads of small white flowers, spread evenly over the tree. The flowers have a pleasant smell. The familiar clusters of red pea-sized berries form in August and look very decorative against the orangey-yellow of the autumn leaves.

How to grow

Height Up to 10m (30ft)
Habitat A very adaptable tree, the rowan will grow just about anywhere.
Garden care As long as it does not get too hot for long in the early months, the rowan will look after itself once established.
Propagation Bare-rooted or pot-grown saplings of the native tree or the several cultivars are easily available from garden centres and nurseries. Bare-rooted trees are best planted in autumn or in a mild spell in winter. Cuttings can be taken in summer or autumn. The berries can be picked and sown in a pot to germinate in spring.

◀ **Rowan**
(*Sorbus aucuparia*)

Lathyrus sylvestris
Sweet pea (everlasting)

Description

THE NARROW-LEAVED everlasting sweet pea is just one of several closely related and fairly similar perennial sweet peas that are native to this country. They are more scrambling than truly climbing like the annual garden varieties. Their large, showy flowers are pink to purple in colour, sometimes with white markings on the lower petals and held in long-stalked loose bunches of three to six flowers during July and August. They naturally scramble over shrubs or sprawl over the ground, but will happily make their way up and along a picket fence or up the side of an arch through another climber, such as an early-flowering clematis.

How to grow

Height Up to 2m (6ft)
Habitat Open woodland and scrub.
Garden care Provide a suitable support and plenty of sun, deadhead often or pick the flowers for the vase and these plants will reward you with a prolific show of flowers during the season.
Propagation Seed and sometimes plants of the everlasting pea are available from the local garden centre. The other species can be obtained from specialist nurseries. Seed needs to be scarified (the coat scratched) before sowing in late summer or early autumn in pots which can be kept outside.

▶ **Everlasting sweet pea (*Lathyrus sylvestris*)**

Vicia cracca
Vetch (tufted)

Description

ARGUABLY THE most handsome of three closely related species, the tufted vetch is also the tallest, climbing up to around 2m (6ft) through hedges and shrubs and throwing out flower spikes on side branches as it goes. The flowers are bluish purple: there are up to 40 flowers on a spike that can be up to 7.5cm (3in) long. The leaves are divided, in the manner of many of the pea family, into a double row of definite ovate leaflets, anything from ten to thirty per leaf. The leaf tips bear branched tendrils, with which the plant climbs. It nearest relatives are the wood vetch (*V. sylvatica*) and the bush vetch (*V. sepium*). All three are perennial, growing from a rhizome or underground stem.

How to grow

Height Up to 2m (6ft)
Habitat Hedgerows, open scrub and rough grassland
Garden care Water in well when planting and deadhead to extend flowering, which can last from early June into September.
Propagation Seed and plants are available from specialist nurseries. Seed can be saved from existing plants and needs scarifying (or scratching of the outer coat), before being sown either in autumn or spring in pots or where it is to flower. Plants can be lifted and divided every three years or so.

◀ **Tufted vetch (*Vicia cracca*)**

Lathyrus pratensis
Vetchling (meadow)

Description

THIS WEAKLY climbing perennial has round heads of up to 12 yellow pea–like flowers, about 2.5cm (1in) long, from May to August, followed by narrow, black seed pods. The vetchlings differ from the vetches in having just a few leaflets, arising from a central point, instead of several leaflets borne in a ladder–like arrangement. There are ten species native to the British Isles, with flowers of pink, red and white, and yellow. The meadow vetchling is by far the most common, forming bright patches of yellow in tall grassland through the summer. It climbs and scrambles by twining tendrils in the same way as vetches and sweet peas, to which it is closely related.

How to grow

Height Up to 1.2m (4ft) with sufficient support.
Habitat Dry grassland, scrub and woodland edges.
Garden care Water in well when planting, placing the plant close to some support, be it grasses or other plants. Deadhead to extend flowering season and cut back hard in September. A feed with well-rotted manure or other organic fertilizer in spring will give vigour and strength.
Propagation Seed is available from specialist nurseries or can be saved from existing plants and sown in pots in autumn. It needs to be scarified before sowing; that is, the surface of the seed needs to be scratched to aid germination.

▶ **Meadow vetchling (*Lathyrus pratensis*)**

Sorbus aria
Whitebeam

Description

THIS SMALL to medium–sized tree is highly decorative for much of the year and can withstand dry conditions, pollution and salt winds. The 'beam' part of the name is simply Saxon for tree; the leaves that give it the other part of its name are fairly large and elliptical, with fine teeth along the edges and white down underneath. The top sides of the leaves are pale in spring, darkening with maturity, then in autumn turning a rich russet colour along with the scarlet red of the berries. The sweet-scented white flowers, borne in large, tight bunches at the tips of the twigs, appear in April and May.

How to grow

Height Up to 13m (45ft), but often smaller, with a neat, compact habit.
Habitat Naturally grows in open woodland, generally on chalk or limestone soils. Also thrives on sunny slopes and dry soils.
Garden care It will benefit from a low stake when young. It can be pruned to size once a year, preferably in early spring just before the sap rises, as it flowers on the current year's growth.
Propagation Young trees are available from nurseries and garden centres and can be planted at any time of year. Bare-root plants are best planted in winter. Semi-ripe cuttings can be taken in late summer and potted in a sheltered spot.

◀ **Whitebeam (*Sorbus aria*)**

Salix caprea
Willow (pussy)

Description

A TREE OF many names, the pussy willow is also known as the goat willow, goat palm or sallow. Uniquely among British willows, the pussy willow has broad, ovate leaves. These are a bluish green in colour and the undersides felted with fine white hairs. The leaves appear after the catkins, which bloom in March and April. There are male and female trees and it is the females which gave the tree its popular name, for though they are less conspicuous than the males their catkins are larger and, once fertilized, covered with a dense coat of silver hair.

How to grow

Height Rarely exceeds 10m (30ft) in height.
Habitat Woodland edges, in clearings and on slopes, it is most at home on damp soil, especially beside open water or in a ditch or stream.
Garden care Staking is unlikely to be needed. The young shoot tips can be prone to attack by blackfly in summer. A spray of soapy water or if the infestation is bad, a proprietary aphid spray should deal with these.
Propagation Plants are available from nurseries and garden centres. Cuttings 30cm (12in) long can be pushed into the ground after stripping the majority, though not all, of the leaves. Seed can be sown if you have a female tree. Sow in damp sterile compost in late spring and pot on when large enough to handle. Germination rate is usually very good.

▶ **Pussy willow (*Salix caprea*)**

Taxus baccata
Yew (common)

Description

O NE OF only three native conifers in Britain, the common yew is the one found in southern parts, while the Scots pine (*Pinus sylvestris*) and the juniper (p127) are generally found naturally in northern England and Scotland. The common yew is noted for its great longevity and slow growth. The yew is a useful hedging or topiary plant, the dense coating of dark leaflets, held in opposite pairs on the narrow, pliable stems lending themselves well to close clipping. The thin, reddish bark, the needles once they are clipped, and the seed are all poisonous to humans and animals, though the flesh of the bright-red berries is not. If allowed, the common yew will not grow excessively large, though the trunk will become wide and gnarled.

How to grow

Height No more than 16m (52ft), even at an old age, but can be clipped.
Habitat Mainly found on chalk or limestone soils. Can tolerate quite deep shade.
Garden care The tree flowers in February and the berries appear in autumn, so any clipping must take this into account.
Propagation Saplings are available from nurseries and some garden centres. Pencil-thick to finger-thick cuttings can be taken.

◀ **Common yew (*Taxus baccata*)**

Further reading

THERE ARE many sources of information on British wildflowers and on gardening with them, but among the best are:

Flora Britannica, Richard Mabey
(Chatto and Windus, 1996, ISBN: 9781856193771)

Every Day Gardening in Colour, Percy Thrower
(Hamlyn, 1985, ISBN: 9780600442424)

How to Make a Wildlife Garden, Chris Baines
(Elm Tree Books, 1985, ISBN: 9780241114483)

Wild Flowers of Britain and Europe, W. Lippert and D. Podlech (Collins, 1994, ISBN: 9780002199964)

Field Guide to the Trees and Shrubs of Britain
(Reader's Digest, 2001, ISBN: 9780276425073)

The AA Book of the British Countryside
(Hodder and Stoughton, 1973, ISBN: 0903356112)

There is also a wealth of information on the Internet, some of it put there by specialist nurseries, some by other interested parties. A huge list of British wild flower species is to be found on the Natural History Museum website, **www.nhm.ac.uk/nature-online/life/plants-fungi**.

For information on specific plants, Wikipedia has an enormous database at **www.wikipedia.org** Many of the places mentioned opposite have their own websites, as do most suppliers of wildflower seeds and plants. The most important source of information on this and related topics remains your own senses. You need to get out there, in your own garden or someone else's or into the countryside and see, hear, smell and feel the plants and watch the wildlife that they attract.

Places to visit

MANY SPECIALIST nurseries and plant centres including: Bridgemere Garden World and Stapeley Water Gardens, both near Nantwich in Cheshire, the Naturescape Wildflower Farm in Langar, Notts, Barncroft Nurseries in Longdon, Staffs, The Water Garden in Hinton Parva near Swindon, Wilts and Eastgrove Cottage Garden Nursery, Sankyns Green in Worcestershire have display gardens laid out to provide inspiration for your own planting schemes. The late Geoff Hamilton's garden at Barnsdale, Exton Near Oakham in Rutland, the Beth Chatto Gardens at Elmstead Market, Chelmsford, Essex, the Water Gardens at Wembworthy, Chumleigh in Devon, Brook Cottage garden in Alkerton near Banbury, Oxfordshire, Bro Meigan Gardens, Boncath, Pembrokeshire and the RHS gardens at Wisley in Surrey, Rosemoor in North Devon and Harlow Carr near Harrogate in Yorkshire are all truly inspirational.

The National Gardens Scheme have details of local gardens opening for charity in their Yellow Book, copies of which are commonly available at your local garden centre. The local press often carries this information too. English Heritage and the National Trust own many properties including nature reserves and beauty spots that are well worth visiting.

The Woodland Trust also owns and manages many nature reserves throughout the country that are open to the public. Then there are the local wildlife trusts, the details of which should be available through your local library or the Internet, which own and operate many small reserves. All these and many more places are worth seeing, both for inspiration and to see what grows naturally in your area.

Index

Page numbers in **bold**
include illustrations.

A

Acer
  A. campestre 119, 159, **164**
  A. platanoides 164
  A. pseudoplatanus 164
Achillea millefolium **73**
Aconitum napellus **26**, **77**
Adonis
  A. annua **54**, **56**, **67**
  A. flammea 67
Agrostemma githago 54
Ajuga reptans 10, 35, **116**, 136,
  138, 139, 144
Alchemilla
  A. mollis 23
  A. vulgaris 15, **23**, **136**, 138
alder (*Alnus glutinosa*) **160**
Alisma plantago-aquatica **98**,
  100, **112**
Alliaria petiolata **156**
Allium
  A. schoenoprasum 9, 10, **19**,
    76, **97**
  A. sphaerocephalum 57
  A. ursinum 10, 136, **149**
Alnus glutinosa **160**
Althea officinalis 24, **77**
Anagallis
  A. arvensis **34**, **35**, **36**, **43**, **54**
  A. tenella 79, **89**
Anemone nemorosa 136, **137**, **140**
Anthemis
  A. arvensis 54, **60**
  A. cotula 60
  A. nobilis 34, 60
  A. tinctoria **34**
Anthriscus sylvestris **56**, **57**, 69
Aquilegia vulgaris 15, **20**
Arabis Hirsuta **36**
Arctostaphylos Uva-Ursi 35, **118**
Armeria maritima **34**, **49**, **96**
arrowhead (*Sagittaria sagittifolia*)
  98, **100**
Artemesia
  A. absinthum **133**, 139
  A. maritima 133
Arum maculatum **96**, 99, **136**,
  137, **145**
ash (*Fraxinus excelsior*) 123, **160**
Asplenium ceterach **34**
Astragalus boeticus 57
Astrantia major **25**
Athyrium filix-femina **11**
Atropa belladonna 141, 167
Avena fatua **63**
avens
  water (*Geum rivale*) **76**, **80**
  wood (*Geum urbanum*) 80, **138**

B

barberry (*Berberis vulgaris*) **117**, **120**
bare-rooted plants 117, 156, 157–158
basil, wild (*Clinopodium vulgare*)
  16, 88
bearberry (*Arctostaphylos Uva-Ursi*)
  35, **118**
bedstraw (*Galium*) **58**, 58, **136**, **152**
beech (*Fagus*) **116**, **118**, 159,
  161, 165
bell-heather (*Erica cinerea*) **118**
Bellis perennis **41**, 56
Berberis vulgaris **117**, **120**
betony (*Stachys officinalis*) 93
Betula pendula **157**
bird's-eye primroses (*Primula
  farinosa*) **14**, 79
bird's-foot trefoil (*Lotus*) **36**, 37, **38**,
  57, **81**
bistort (*Polygonum*) **15**, **18**, **96**,
  97, **98**, 99
black nightshade (*Solanum
  nigrum*) 167
blackthorn (*Prunus spinosa*)
  118, **120**, 159
bladderwort (*Utricularia vulgaris*) **101**
bluebells (*Hyacinthoides non-
  scripta*) **15**, **116**, 136, **137**,
  140, 149, 153
bog arum (*Calla palustris*) **98**, **100**
bog asphodel (*Narthecium
  ossifragum*) **76**, **78**, **81**
bog gardens 76–79
  plant directory **80–93**
bog myrtle (*Myrica gale*) 78
bog rush (*Schoenus nigricans*) **106**
bogbean (*Menyanthes trifoliata*)
  98, **101**
bonsai 159
box (*Buxus sempervirens*) **117**,
  118, **119**, 139
Briza media **63**
brooklime (*Veronica beccabunga*)
  79, 108
broom (*Cytisus scoparius*) **15**, **34**,
  118, **121**
buddleia (*Buddleja davidii*) **15**
bugle (*Ajuga reptans*) 10, 35, **116**,
  136, **138**, 139, 144
bulbs, propagation 16
bur-reed, branched (*Sparganium
  erectum*) **102**
burnet rose (*Rosa pimpinellifolia*) 118
butcher's broom (*Ruscus aculeatus*)
  16, 119, **121**, 139
Butomus umbellatus **97**, **107**
butterbur (*Petasites hybridus*) **82**
buttercup (*Ranunculus sp.*) 54, 57,
  58, 58, 110
butterwort, common (*Pinguicula
  vulgaris*) **76**, 79
Buxus sempervirens **117**, **118**,
  119, 139

C

Calamagrostis epigeios (wood
  small-read) **92**
Calla palustris **98**, **100**
Callitriche palustris **109**
Calluna vulgaris **35**, **96**, **118**, **126**
Caltha palustris **77**, **87**, **96**
Calystegia soldanella **34**
Campanula
  C. patula 35, 37, **38**
  C. rotundifolia **22**, **34**, **36**
  C. trachelium **27**
campions (*Silene*) **14**, **34**, 37, **39**,
  55, **57**, **59**, 136, 149
Canadian pondweed (*Elodea
  canadensis*) 99
Cardamine pratensis **85**
Carex
  C. pendula 99, 139, **146**
  C. riparia **104**
  C. sylvatica 139, **153**
Carpinus betulus 159, **165**
celandine, lesser (*Ranunculus
  ficaria*) **18**
Centaurea
  C. cyanus **54**, 57, **60**
  C. montana 63
  C. nigra 57, **65**
  C. scabiosa **15**, 65
Centaurium erythraea **39**
centaury (*Centaurium*) **39**
Centranthus ruber 58
Cerastium arvense 151
chamomile (*Anthemis*) **34**, 54, **60**
cherry (*Prunus*) **116**, 159, **161**,
  162
chicory (*Cichorium intybus*) **55**, 57
chives (*Allium schoenoprasum*) 9,
  10, **19**, **76**, **97**
Chrysanthemum
  C. leucanthemum (see
    Leucanthemum vulgare)
  C. parthenium **17**, **21**, 34
  C. segetum **54**, **55**, 57, **65**
Cichorium intybus **55**, 57
Circaea lutetiana **141**
Clematis vitalba 139, 159, **168**
climbers 16, 139, **156**, 159
  plant directory **160–171**
Clinopodium vulgare 16, 88
clover (*Trifolium*) **54**, 57
Cochlearia officinalis **46**, 79
colour, use of 10–11
columbine (*Aquilegia vulgaris*)
  15, **20**
comfrey (*Symphytum officinale*)
  82, 99
Conium maculatum (hemlock) 69
containers (see also rockeries)
  37, 77, 78, 96, 159
Convallaria majalis **14**, 37, **145**, 149
corn cockle (*Agrostemma
  githago*) 54

corn marigolds (*Chrysanthemum
  segetum*) **54**, **55**, 57, **65**
cornflowers (*Centaurea*) **54**, 57,
  60, 63
Cornus sanguinea **96**, **116**, **118**,
  122, 160
Corydalis lutea **35**, 37, 139
Corylus avellana **126**
  'Spiralis' **91**
cotton grass (*Eriophorum
  angustifolium*) **83**
cow parsley (*Anthriscus sylvestris*)
  56, **57**, **69**
cowslip (*Primula veris*) 54, **55**, 56,
  57, **61**
crab apple (*Malus sylvestris*) **157**,
  163
cranberry (*Vaccinium oxycoccos*)
  78, **118**
cranesbills (*Geranium*) **14**, **15**, **16**,
  21, 27, **40**, 54, **56**, **61**, 138
Crataegus
  C. laevigata 125
  C. monogyna 118, 119, **125**,
    157, 159
creeping bellflowers (*Campanula
  patula*) **35**, 37, **38**
creeping cinquefoil (*Potentilla
  reptans*) **35**, **40**
creeping Jenny (*Lysimachia
  nummularia*) **76**, 78, 79, **83**, 147
Crepis
  C. biennis 64
  C. capillaris 64
  C. vesicaria 57, **64**
crested dog's tail (*Cymosurus
  cristatus*) **63**
cross-leaved heath (*Erica tetralix*)
  76, 78, **118**
cuckoo flower (*Cardamine
  pratensis*) 88
cyclamen (*Hederifolium
  purpurescens*) **137**, **138**, 139
Cymosurus cristatus **62**
Cytisus scoparius **15**, **34**, **118**, **121**

D

daffodil (*Narcissus pseudonarcissus*)
  16, 56, 136, **141**
daisies (*Bellis perennis*) **41**, 56
Daphne mezereum 16, **118**,
  128, 139
dead nettle, white (*Lamium album*) 153
deadly nightshade (*Atropa
  belladonna*) 141, 167
devil's-bit scabious (*Succisa
  pratensis*) **34**, **45**
Dianthus
  D. deltoides **34**, **43**
  D. gratianopolitanus **36**, 43
Digitalis purpurea **15**, **17**, **117**,
  136, **138**, **143**
Dipsacus fullonum **71**

dogwood (*Cornus sanguinea*) **96**, **116**, **118**, **122**, 160
Draba aizoides **51**
dropwort (*Filipendula vulgaris*) 88
Drosera rotundifolia 76
Dryas octopetala 80
Dryopteris felix-mas **96**, **137**, **142**

E

Echium vulgare 15, **16**, **31**
elder (*Sambucus nigra*) **123**
Eleocharis
  E. acicularis **104**
  E. palustris **106**
Elodea canadensis 99
enchanter's nightshade (*Circaea lutetiana*) **141**
Epilobium
  E. angustifolium 77, **90**, **97**
  E. hirsutum 90
  E. montanum 90
Eranthis hyemalis 138
Erica
  E. cinerea **118**
  E. tetralix **76**, 78, **118**
Eriophorum angustifolium **83**
Erodium cicutarium **14**, 35, **36**, 37
Eryngium maritimum **28**, 79
Eryngo *E. campestre* 28
Erysimum cheiranthoides 16
Euonymus europaea 118, **130**
Eupatorium cannabinum **79**
Euphorbia amygdaloides **130**, 139
everlasting sweet pea (*Lathyrus sylvestris*) 16, 159, **169**

F

Fagus
  F. purpurea **116**, **118**, **161**
  F. sylvatica 159, **161**, 165
feather grass, common (*Stipa pennata*) **63**
ferns 11, **15**, **17**, 77, **96**, 99, **137**, **138**, 139, **142**
feverfew (*Chrysanthemum parthenium*) **17**, **21**, 34
field hollies (*Eryngo E. campestre*) 28
field maple (*Acer campestre*) 119, 159, **164**
field mousear (*Cerastium arvense*) 151
field scabious (*Knautia arvensis*) **70**
figwort 79, **84**
Filipendula
  F. ulmaria **16**, **77**, 78, **79**, **88**
  F. vulgaris 88
fleabane, common (*Pulicaria dysenterica*) **76**, 77, **78**, **90**
flowering rush (*Butomus umbellatus*) **97**, **107**
forget-me-nots (*Myosotis*) **14**, **77**, 79, 99, **102**, **142**
foxgloves (*Digitalis purpurea*) **15**, **17**, **117**, 136, **138**, **143**
Fragaria vesca **49**, 79
Fraxinus excelsior 123, **160**
Fritillaria meleagris 16, **55**, 56
frogbit (*Hydrocharis morsus-ranae*) **98**, 99, **103**
fumitory (*Fumaria officinalis*) 16, 37

G

Galanthus 138, 149, **149**
Galium
  G. aparine 58
  G. mollugo 58
  G. odoratum 58, **136**, **152**
  G. verum **58**
garlic, wild (*Allium ursinum*) 136, **149**
Gentiana 31, 79
  G. amarella 35, **36**
  G. cilliata 35
  G. pneumonanthe **76**, **77**
  G. verna 35
gentians (*Gentiana*) 31, 35, **36**, **76**, **77**, 79
Geranium
  G. dissectum 40
  G. molle **40**
  G. pratense **15**, **16**, **56**, **61**
  G. pusillum 40
  G. robertianum **144**
  G. sanguineum **14**, **21**, 27
  G. sylvaticum 61, **138**
Gerard, John 132
Geum
  G. rivale **76**, **80**
  G. urbanum 80, **138**
Gladiolus palustris 76
globe flower (*Trollius europaeus*) **85**
Glyceria maxima 79, **105**
golden marjoram (*O. vulgare* 'Aureum') 25
goldenrod (*Solidago virgaurea*) 15, 58, 67
goose grass (*Galium aparine*) 58
gorse (*Ulex*) **116**, 118, 119, 123, **123**
grape hyacinth (*Muscari*) **14**, 16, 22, **22**
grasses 35, 57, 62–63, 78, **117**, 139
great burnet (*Sanguisorba officinalis*) **54**
ground cover plants 10, 16, 133
guelder rose (*Viburnum opulus*) 118, **124**, **157**

H

hairy rock cress (*Arabis Hirsuta*) **36**
harebells (*Campanula rotundifolia*) **22**, **34**, **36**
hart's tongue (*Phyllitis scolopendrium*) 139
hawk's beard (*Crepis*) 57, **64**, 64
hawthorn (*Crataegus*) 118, 119, **125**, **157**, 159
hazel (*Corylus avellana*) **91**, **126**
heartsease (*Viola tricolor*) 31, **41**
heather (*Calluna vulgaris*) **35**, **96**, **118**, **126**
Hedera helix 16, 139, 159, **166**
Hederifolium purpurescens **137**, **138**, 139
hedging 119
Helianthemum
  H. apenninum 44, **118**
  H. canum 44
  H. nummularium **16**, **17**, **34**, 35, **36**, **44**, 79, **118**
hellebores (*Helleborus*)

H. foetidus **137**, **151**
  H. niger 151
  H. orientalis 151
  H. viridis 151
hemlock (*Conium maculatum*) 69
hemp agrimony (*Eupatorium cannabinum*) **79**
herb paris (*Paris quadrifolia*) **138**
herb Robert (*Geranium robertianum*) **144**
Hidcote, Gloucestershire 15
Hippophae rhamnoides 118
holly (*Ilex aquifolium*) **116**, **117**, 118, **127**, 139, 159
honeysuckle (*Lonicera periclymenum*) 16, 139, **156**, 159, **164**
hops (*Humulus lupulus*) 159, **165**, 166
hornbeam (*Carpinus betulus*) 159, **165**
hostas (*Hosta*) 99
Hottonia palustris 99
Humulus lupulus 159, **165**, 166
Hyacinthoides non-scripta **15**, **116**, 136, **137**, **140**, 149, 153
Hydrocharis morsus-ranae **98**, 99, **103**
Hydrocotyle vulgaris **78**
hyper-tufa 37
Hypericum sp. **16**, **30**, 57
  H. androsaenum **131**, 139
  H. hirsutum 30
  H. perforatum 30
  H. pulchrum 30
  H. tetrapterum 30

I, J

Ilex aquifolium **116**, **117**, 118, **127**, 139, 159
Iris
  I. foetidissima 113, 139
  I. pseudacorus **78**, 79, **96**, **97**, 102, **113**
ivy (*Hedera helix*) 16, 139, 159, **166**
Jack-by-the-hedge (*Alliaria petiolata*) **156**
Jacob's ladder (*Polemonium caeruleum*) 15, **23**
Jasione montana **29**
Juncus
  J. conglomeratus **106**, 107
  J. effusus **91**
  J. filiformis **107**
juniper, common (*Juniper communis*) **117**, **118**, **119**, **127**, 171

K, L

knapweed (*Centaurea*) **15**, 57, **65**
Knautia arvensis **70**
lady fern (*Athyrium filix-femina*) **11**
lady's mantle (*Alchemilla*) 15, **23**, **136**, 138
lady's smock (*Cardamine pratensis*) **85**
lamb's ears (*Stachys lantana*) 93
Lamiastrum galeobdolon **153**
Lamium album (white dead nettle) 153

Lathyrus
  L. pratensis 57, 72, **170**
  L. sylvestris 16, 159, **169**
  L. vernus 72
layering 119
Leucanthemum vulgare 38, 54, **56**, 57, **66**
Ligustrum
  L. ovalifolium 129
  L. vulgare **96**, 119, **129**
Lilium martagon 16
lily of the valley (*Convallaria majalis*) **14**, 37, **145**, 149
lime (*Tilia*) 159, **166**
Linaria
  L. cymbalaria **35**, 37
  L. vulgaris 15–16, **31**
Lonicera periclymenum 16, 139, **156**, 159, **164**
loosestrife **79**, **86–87**, 90
lords and ladies (*Arum maculatum*) **96**, 99, **136**, **137**, **145**
Lotus
  L. corniculatus **36**, 37, **38**
  L. uliginosus 57, **81**
lungwort (*Pulmonaria officinalis*) 136, **146**
Lychnis
  L. flos-cuculi **76**, **77**, **89**, **96**
  L. viscaria 35
Lysimachia
  L. nemorum **147**
  L. nummularia **76**, 78, 79, **83**, 147
  L. vulgaris 27, 67, **77**, 78, **87**, **96**, 147
Lythrum salicaria 67, **79**, **86**, 90, **96**

M

Maianthemum bifolium 139
male fern (*Dryopteris felix-mas*) **96**, **137**, **142**
mallow (*Malva*) 15, **24**, 57, 79
Malus sylvestris **157**, **163**
Malva
  M. alcea 24
  M. neglecta 24
  M. moschata **24**, 57, 79
  M. sylvestris 15, **24**
marigolds **54**, **65**, **77**
marjoram (*Origanum vulgare*) 15, 16, **25**, 35, 88
marsh gladiolus (*Gladiolus palustris*) 76
marsh mallow (*Althea officinalis*) 24, **77**
marsh marigolds (*Caltha palustris*) **77**, **87**, **96**
marsh pennywort (*Hydrocotyle vulgaris*) **78**
marsh trefoil (*Menyanthes trifoliate*) **79**
marsh valerian (*Valeriana dioica*) **77**
marsh violet (*Viola palustris*) 79
marsh woundwort (*Stachys palustris*) 79, **93**
marshes and bogs 75–93
martagon lily (*Lilium martagon*) 16
masterwort (*Astrantia major*) **25**
Matricaria discoidea **16**
Matteuccia struthiopteris 77
may lilies (*Maianthemum bifolium*) 139
meadow buttercup (*Ranunculus acris*) **56**, 58

meadow clary (*Salvia pratensis*) 54, 57
meadow grass, wood (*Poa nemoralis*) **62**
meadow rue (*Thalictrum*) **96**
meadow vetchling (*Lathyrus pratensis*) 57, 72, **170**
meadows 54–57
  plant directory **58–73**
meadowsweet (*Filipendula ulmaria*) **16**, **77**, 78, **79**, **88**
Meconopsis cambrica **16**, **34**, **147**
Melilotus officinalis **8**
Mentha aquatica 84, **88**, 139
Menyanthes trifoliata **98**, **101**
mezereon (*Daphne mezereum*) 16, **118**, **128**, 139
mignonette (*Reseda*) **14**, **15**, **26**
milk parsley (*Peucedanum palustre*) **78**
milk vetch (*Astragalus boeticus*) 57
milkwort, common (*Polygala vulgaris*) **36**
mint, water (*Mentha aquatica*) 84, **88**
mixed borders 14–17
  plant directory **18–31**
monkshood (*Aconitum napellus*) **26**, **77**
mossy saxifrage (*Saxifraga hypnoides*) **44**
mountain ash (*Sorbus aucuparia*) 160
mountain avens (*Dryas octopetala*) 80
mowing meadows 54, 55, 56, 57
mullein (*Verbascum*) **55**, 58, 66, **66**, 66
Muscari
  M. botryoides 22
  M. neglectum **14**, 16, **22**
musk mallow (*Malva moschata*) **24**, 57, 79
Myosotis
  M. alpestris 142
  M. arvensis **14**, **77**, 142
  M. scorpioides 79, 99, **102**
  M. sylvatica **142**
Myrica gale 78
Myriophyllum spicatum 99

N

Narcissus pseudonarcissus 16, 56, 136, **141**
Narthecium ossifragum **76**, **78**, **81**
Nasturtium
  N. microphyllum 109
  N. officinale **109**
navelwort (*Umbilicus rupestris*) **16**, 34, **42**
needle spike rush (*Eleocharis acicularis*) **104**
nettle-leaved bellflowers (*Campanula trachelium*) **27**
Norway maple (*Acer platanoides*) 164
Nuphar lutea **97**, **112**
Nymphaea alba **98**, **111**
Nymphoides peltata 99, **103**

O

oak 159, **167**
old man's beard (*Clematis vitalba*) 139, 159, **168**

Onobrychis viciifolia 38, 54, **56**, 57, **70**
Ononis
  O. repens **69**, 79
  O. spinosa 69
orchids, wild 79
Origanum vulgare 15, 16, **25**, 35, 88
orpine (*Sedum telephium*) **138**, 139
ox-eye daisies (*Leucanthemum vulgare*) 38, 54, **56**, 57, **66**
Oxalis acetosella 37, **150**
oxlip (*Primula elatior*) 61
oxygenating plants 99

P

Papaver **54**
  P. argemone 68
  P. dubium 68
  P. hybridum 68
  P. rhoeas 15, **54**, 57, **68**
Paris quadrifolia **138**
parsley, wild **8**
parsnip, wild (*Pastinaca sativa*) 58, **67**
pasque flower (*Pulsatilla vulgaris*) **34**, **42**
Pastinaca sativa 58, **67**
patios, mid-summer **35**
periwinkle (*Vinca sp.*) **96**, **128**, 136, 139
Petasites hybridus **82**
Peucedanum palustre **78**
pheasant's eye (Adonis) **54**, **56**, **67**, 67
Phyllitis scolopendrium 139
pimpernels (*Anagallis*) **34**, **35**, **36**, **43**, **54**, 79, **89**
pineappleweed (*Matricaria discoidea*) **16**
Pinguicula vulgaris **76**, 79
pinks (*Dianthus*) **34**, **36**, 43, **43**
Pinus sylvestris 159, 171
Plantago lanceolata **15**
plantain ribwort (*Plantago lanceolata*) **15**
Poa nemoralis 35, **62**
poisonous plants **26**, 69, **92**, **100**, **108**, **124**, **128**, **167**, **171**
Polemonium caeruleum 15, **23**
Polygala vulgaris **36**
Polygonatum
  P. multiflorum **136**, **150**
  P. odoratum 150
Polygonum
  P. amphibium **96**, **97**, **98**, 99
  P. bistorta **15**, **18**, **96**
ponds 96–99
  plant directory **100–113**
poppies 15, **34**, **54**, **56**, 57, **68**, **147**
pot-grown trees 156, 157–158
Potentilla
  P. anserina **46**
  P. erecta **40**
  P. reptans 35, **40**
potted plants **117**
primroses (*Primula vulgaris*)
  P. elatior 61
  P. farinosa **14**, 79
  P. veris 54, **55**, 56, 57, **61**
  P. vulgaris **14**, 37, 136, **148**

privet (*Ligustrum*) **96**, 119, **129**
propagation (see also *plant listings*) 16–17, 119, 159
Prunella vulgaris 16, **28**
Prunus
  P. avium **162**
  P. cerasifera 159, **162**
  P. padus **116**, **161**
  P. spinosa 118, **120**, 159
Pulicaria dysenterica **76**, 77, **78**, **90**
Pulmonaria
  P. longifolia 146
  P. officinalis **136**, **146**
Pulsatilla vulgaris **34**, **42**
purple loosestrife (*Lythrum salicaria*) 67, **79**, **86**, 90, **96**

Q, R

quaking grass (*Briza media*) **63**
Queen Anne's lace (*Anthriscus sylvestris*) **56**, **57**, **69**
Quercus
  Q. petraea 167
  Q. robur 159, **167**
ragged robin (*Lychnis flos-cuculi*) **76**, **77**, 88, **89**, **96**
ragwort (*Senecio jacobaea*) **8**
'rain-shadow' effect 137
ramsons (*Allium ursinum*) 10, 136, **149**
Ranunculus 54, 57, **58**
  R. aconitifolius 110
  R. acris **56**, 58
  R. aquatilis **98**, **110**
  R. bulbosa 58
  R. ficaria **18**
  R. flammula **92**
  R. fluitans 110
  R. lingua 92, **108**
  R. repens 58
red valerian (*Centranthus ruber*) 58
reed sweet-grass (*Glyceria maxima*) 79, **105**
reedmace (*Typha latifolia*) **78**, 102, **105**
Reseda lutea **14**, 15, **26**
Reseda luteola 26
Reseda odorata 26
restharrow (*Ononis*) **69**, **79**
ribbed melilot (*Melilotus officinalis*) **8**
river water crowfoot (*Ranunculus fluitans*) 110
rockeries 34–37
  plant directory **38–51**
rockrose (*Helianthemum nummularium*) **16**, **17**, **34**, 35, **36**, **44**, 79, **118**
roses (*Rosa*) **122**, **156**
  R. arvensis **122**
  R. canina **122**, 156
  R. pimpinellifolia 118, **129**
  R. rubiginosa 118, **131**
round-headed leeks (*Allium sphaerocephalum*) 57
round-leaved sundew (*Drosera rotundifolia*) 76
rowan (*Sorbus aucuparia*) 160, **168**
Rumex acetosella 57
Ruscus aculeatus 16, 119, **121**, 139
rushes (*Juncus*) 62, 78, **91**, **104**, **106–107**
rusty back fern (*Asplenium ceterach*) **34**

S

Sagittaria sagittifolia **98**, **100**
sainfoin (*Onobrychis viciifolia*) 38, 54, **56**, 57, **70**
Salix **119**
  S. alba 159
  S. caprea **171**
Salvia pratensis 54, 57
Sambucus nigra **123**
Sanguisorba officinalis **54**
Saponaria officinalis **36**
Saxifraga hypnoides **44**
saxifrage, mossy (*Saxifraga hypnoides*) **44**
Scabiosa columbaria 45, 70
scabious (*Scabiosa*) **45**, 70
Schoenus nigricans **106**
Scots pine (*Pinus sylvestris*) 159, 171
Scrophularia
  S. auriculata 84
  S. nodosa 79, **84**
scurvy grass (*Cochlearia officinalis*) **46**, 79
sea bindweed (*Calystegia soldanella*) **34**
sea buckthorn (*Hippophae rhamnoides*) 118
sea hollies (*Eryngium maritimum*) **28**, **79**
sea wormwood (*Artemesia maritima*) 133
seasonal planting 10, **14**, **15**, **16**
sedges (*Carex*) 62, 99, **104**, 139, **146**, **153**
Sedum
  S. acre 35, **36**, **48**
  S. album 48
  S. anglicum **48**
  S. dasyphyllum **35**
  S. telephium **138**, 139
seeds 16–17
self-heal (*Prunella vulgaris*) 16, **28**
Senecio jacobaea **8**
sensory gardens 10, 133
shade 136–139
  plant directory **140–153**
Sheep's-bit (*Jasione montana*) **29**
sheep's sorrel (*Rumex acetosella*) 57
shrubs 116–119
  plant directory **120–133**
shuttlecock ferns (*Matteuccia struthiopteris*) 77
Silene
  S. alba **14**, **59**
  S. dioica **55**, **57**, **59**, 136, 149
  S. uniflora **34**, 37, **39**
  S. vulgaris **39**, 59
silver birch (*Betula pendula*) **157**
silverweed (*Potentilla anserina*) **46**
snake's-head fritillary (*Fritillaria meleagris*) 16, **55**, 56
snowdrops (*Galanthus*) 138, 149, **149**
soapwort (*Saponaria officinalis*) **36**
soil enrichment 17, 57, 137
Solanum
  S. dulcamara 141, **167**
  S. nigrum 167
Solidago virgaurea 15, 58, 67
Solomon's seal (*Polygonatum*) **136**, **150**

Sorbus
  S. aria **157**, 159, **170**
  S. aucuparia 160, **168**
  S. torminalis 124
Sparganium erectum **102**
spearwort (Ranunculus sp.) **92**,
  108
speedwell (Veronica) **15**, **29**, **35**,
  37, **47**, 99, **108**
spike rush, common (Eleocharis
  palustris) **106**
spiked water milfoil (Myriophyllum
  spicatum) 99
spindle tree (Euonymus europaea)
  118, **130**
spring pea (Lathyrus vernus) 72
spurge, wood (Euphorbia
  amygdaloides) **130**
St John's wort (Hypericum sp.)
  30, 57
Stachys
  S. lantana 93
  S. officinalis 93
  S. palustris 79, **93**
  S. sylvatica 93
starwort (Callitriche palustris) **109**
Stellaria
  S. alsine 151
  S. graminea 151
  S. holostea **14**, **151**
sticky catchfly (Lychnis viscaria) 35
stinking iris (Iris foetidissima) 113, 139
Stipa pennata **63**
stitchwort (Stellaria) **14**, **151**, 153
stonecrop (Sedum) **35**, 35, **36**,
  48, 48
storksbill, common (Erodium
  cicutarium) **14**, 35, **36**, 37
Stratiotes aloides **98**, 99, **113**
strawberries, wild (Fragaria vesca)
  49, 79
Succisa pratensis **34**, **45**
sweet gale (Myrica gale) 78
sweet pea, everlasting (Lathyrus
  sylvestris) 16, 167, **169**
sweet woodruff (Galium odoratum)
  58, **152**
sycamore (Acer pseudoplatanus) 164
Symphytum officinale **82**, 99

T

Taxus baccata 159, **171**
teasels (Dipsacus fullonum) **71**
Teucrium scorodonia **138**, 139
Thalictrum **96**
thrift (Armeria maritima) **34**, **49**, **96**
thyme (Thymus) 34, **35**, **50**, 79, 88
  T. praecox 34, **35**, **50**, 79, 88
  T. pulegioides, 50
  T. serpyllum 50
  T. vulgaris 50
Tilia
  T. cordata 166
  T. platyphyllus 166
  T. x europaea 159, **166**
toadflax 15–16, **31**, **35**, 37
tormentil (Potentilla erecta) **40**
treacle mustard (Erysimum
  cheiranthoides) 16
trees 156–159
  plant directory **160–171**
Trifolium
  T. arvense 57
  T. incarnatum **54**
Trollius europaeus **85**, **97**
tutsan (Hypericum androsaenum)
  131, 139
Typha latifolia **78**, 102, **105**

U, V

Ulex
  U. europaeus **116**, 118, 119, **123**
  U. gallii 123
  U. minor 123
Umbilicus rupestris **16**, 34, **42**
Utricularia vulgaris **101**
Vaccinium oxycoccos 78, **118**
valerian, common (Valerianus
  officinalis) **14**, **96**
Valeriana dioica **77**
Valerianus officinalis **14**, **96**
Verbascum
  V. nigrum 66
  V. phoeniceum 66
  V. thapsus **55**, 58, **66**
Verbena officinalis **51**

Veronica
  V. anagallis-aquatica 99, **108**
  V. beccabunga 79, 108
  V. chamaedrys **35**, **47**
  V. filiformis 47
  V. montana 47
  V. officinalis 47
  V. persica 47
  V. scutellata 108
  V. spicata **29**
vervain (Verbena officinalis) **51**
vetch (Vicia) 16, **71**, **72**, 159, **169**
vetchling, meadow (Lathyrus
  pratensis) 57, **170**
Viburnum
  V. lantana 118, **132**
  V. opulus 118, **124**, **157**
Vicia
  V. cracca 159, **169**
  V. sativa 16, **72**
  V. sepium 72, 169
  V. sylvatica 169
Vinca sp. **96**, **128**, 136, 139
Viola
  V. palustris 79
  V. riviniana **15**, 136, **152**
  V. tricolor 31, **41**
Viper's bugloss 15, **16**, **31**
virburnum **117**

W

walls (see also rockeries) 35
water cress (Nasturtium officinale)
  109
water crowfoot (Ranunculus
  aquatilis) **98**, **110**
water features 96
water lilies **97**, **98**, 99, **103**,
  111, **112**
water mint (Mentha aquatica) 84,
  88, 139
water plantain (Alisma plantago-
  aquatica) **98**, 100, **112**
water soldier (Stratiotes aloides)
  98, 99, **113**
water violet (Hottonia palustris) 99
wayfaring tree (Viburnum lantana)
  118, **132**
weld (Reseda luteola) 26
Welsh poppies (Meconopsis
  cambrica) **16**, **34**, **147**
wetland plants 76–79

whitebeam (Sorbus aria) **157**,
  159, **170**
whitlow-grass, yellow (Draba
  aizoides) **51**
wild oat, common (Avena fatua) **63**
wild service tree (Sorbus
  torminalis) 124
willow (Salix) **119**, 159, **171**
willowherb (Epilobium) 77, **90**,
  90, **97**
winter aconite (Eranthis hyemalis) 138
winter cress (Nasturtium
  microphyllum) 109
Wisley, Surrey 15
wood anemone (Anemone
  nemorosa) 136, **137**, **140**
wood meadow grass (Poa
  nemoralis) 35, **62**
wood sage (Teucrium scorodonia)
  138, 139
wood small-reed (Calamagrostis
  epigeios) **92**
wood sorrel (Oxalis acetosella)
  37, **150**
wood spurge (Euphorbia
  amygdaloides) **130**, 139
woodruff, sweet (Galium odoratum)
  58, **136**, **152**
woody nightshade (Solanum
  dulcamara) 141, **167**
wormwood (Artemesia absinthum)
  133, 139
woundwort (Stachys) 79, **93**

Y

yarrow (Achillea millefolium) **73**
yellow archangel (Lamiastrum
  galeobdolon) **153**
yellow flag (Iris pseudacorus) **78**,
  79, **96**, **97**, 102, **113**
yellow fumitory (Corydalis lutea)
  35, 37, 139
yellow loosestrife (Lysimachia
  vulgaris) 27, 67, **77**, 78, **87**,
  96, 147
yellow pimpernel (Lysimachia
  nemorum) **147**
yellow whitlow-grass (Draba
  aizoides) **51**
yew, common (Taxus baccata)
  159, **171**

To place an order or to request a catalogue contact:
GMC Publications
Castle Place, 166 High Street,
Lewes, East Sussex, BN7 1XU
United Kingdom
Tel: +44 (0)1273 488005 Fax: +44 (0)1273 402866
www.gmcbooks.com